Sister to Courage

Stories from the World of Viola Desmond, Canada's Rosa Parks

D1210315

SISTER TO COURAGE

Stories from the World of
Viola Desmond,
Canada's Rosa Parks

by **Wanda Robson**

with **Ronald Caplan**

Breton Books

Sister to Courage © 2010 Wanda Robson

The Publisher wishes to thank Joe Robson for his help while producing *Sister to Courage*.

While they are published here for the first time, readers will be interested to know that some of the stories in this book are part of Wanda Robson's repertoire of public storytelling. They include: "The Christmas Dorothy Died," "My Mother and Clark Gable," "A Walk on the Wild Side," and "I Fly a Kite."

Editor: Ronald Caplan and Bonnie Thompson
Layout: Fader Communications

We acknowledge the support of the Canada Council for the Arts for our publishing program.

 Canada Council for the Arts   Conseil des Arts du Canada

We also acknowledge support from Cultural Affairs, Nova Scotia Department of Tourism, Culture and Heritage.

NOVA SCOTIA
Tourism, Culture and Heritage

We acknowledge the financial support of the Government of Canada through the Canada Book Fund for our publishing activities.

Canadä

Library and Archives Canada Cataloguing in Publication

Robson, Wanda, 1926-
  Sister to courage : stories from the world of Viola Desmond, Canada's Rosa Parks / Wanda Robson with Ronald Caplan.

ISBN 978-1-895415-34-6

  1. Desmond, Viola, 1914-1965. 2. Robson, Wanda, 1926-. 3. Race discrimination--Nova Scotia--History. 4. Civil rights--Nova Scotia--History. 5. Black Canadian women--Nova Scotia--Biography. 6. Businesswomen--Nova Scotia--Biography. 7. Nova Scotia--History--1945-. 8. Halifax (N.S.)--Biography. 9. Nova Scotia--Biography. I. Caplan, Ronald, 1942- II. Title.

FC106.B6R63 2010   971.6'04092   C2010-904374-X

Printed in Canada

Mixed Sources
Product group from well-managed forests and other controlled sources
www.fsc.org Cert no. SW-COC-000952
© 1996 Forest Stewardship Council
FSC

Contents

DEDICATION

**To my husband Joe
and our Children:**

**Sarah Jane Robson
Joseph Gordon Robson
Jeffrey Kevin Neal
Gordon Kenneth Neal
Stephen Alan Neal**

A Little Introduction

WANDA ROBSON COMES FROM a family of fifteen children—an African-Canadian family, with all the complications that implies. Her siblings include the famous pioneer businesswoman and civil rights icon, Viola Desmond. Viola is known today because of one courageous decision on 8 November 1946, when she resisted being moved to the blacks-only section of the Roseland movie theatre in New Glasgow, Nova Scotia. This incident became a significant marker in the struggle for racial equality in Canada.

But Viola was more than a moment in time. She came from the home and family created in Halifax by her parents James Albert Davis and Gwendolyn Irene (Johnson) Davis. This book presents some of the world the Davis family shared, which contributed to Viola's courage not only that one day in 1946 but throughout her life. And while Wanda Robson insists she could never have done what her sister Viola did, this extraordinary book demonstrates that those same principles educated and supported Wanda in raising her own family.

And since Wanda Robson is a storyteller, this book will be a batch of stories from her life.

—Ronald Caplan

CHAPTER ONE

The Christmas Dorothy Died

I OFTEN THINK OF MY PARENTS and the balance they had to endure and navigate, with a very young family and grown children in the same house. In a family as big as ours—fifteen children, eleven that survived—the constant word was "share," and the ongoing struggle my parents had to face was the struggle to maintain balance among all the needs and differences. Almost like a scale for weighing jewels—the kind with two trays on a chain that dip to equal one another—I see the two rooms separated by sliding doors in my parents' house. The living room in front held a bare, undecorated Christmas tree and little children playing, waiting for Santa; and in the parlour on the other side of those doors my parents were preparing the body of their daughter Dorothy, who had just died.

All this had to be told to me. I was the youngest child, just eight days old when Dorothy died, Christ-

1

mas Eve. This happened in 1926. Even though only a story, it seems like my memory, and I imagine my parents at that time, not young and not old—in the middle of so many lives, surrounded by family. Each older sister told some of the story to me later when I was in school. It's a sad story, but years later it was also a story Viola was able to laugh about, as my sisters reminisced. Viola said, "Remember when we came down the street with all the parcels at Christmas!" Then I wanted to know what they were talking about.

And it turns out that it was December 24, 1926. I was eight days old. And I was in a little crib by the bed where my sister Dorothy was. Dorothy was five years old. She wasn't convalescing, she was dying. And my mother knew that, my father knew that. They were told by the doctor six months before, that she had a disease they called peritonitis. I would say it was cancer, perhaps in the stomach lining. The doctor told my mother there was nothing more that they could do for her. My mother would have to get her out in the sun, bare her stomach to the sun. Perhaps that would help. But that was in the late spring or early summer when they told her that. And now it was winter.

I am told Dorothy said when I was born, "Oh, Mama, that will be my baby. Can I take care of her?" And Mum said, "You most certainly can."

My crib was right beside Dorothy's bed. And her bed activities were stringing beads and dressing her doll. My mother kept her doll and the beads.

This was the 24th of December in the house on 18 Swaine Street in Halifax where I was born.

2

The Christmas Dorothy Died

My mother told me: "I was downstairs, stirring soup, getting supper ready." And she said, "I felt I had to go. I felt that there was something wrong." My mother told me this. And one of the girls was in the kitchen. "Where are you going, Mum?" She answered, "It's Dorothy. It's Dorothy." And Mum went into the room, Dorothy's room. I was in there in the crib. And she said Dorothy was sitting up, propped up with the pillows. She had the beads in her hand, where she was stringing them, and the doll by her side. She was dead.

My mother was upset, of course. She had been told of the imminent death. But I don't think a parent is ever fully prepared. You know it, perhaps. Perhaps you don't. But she really was extremely upset. She said, "Call your father, call your father. Somebody go get your father." And Dad came home.

They took Dorothy to the parlour, the rear side of the living room. They were double rooms. A living room here, the front room. I think years ago they called it a front and back parlour. And if something was going on, they had the sliding doors between them. So Dorothy was put in the back parlour.

Our minister came and prayed with Mum. And there was an organ in the corner. And I think—I'm not quite certain about this—I think Mum said she played one of Dorothy's little favourites, like "Jesus Loves Me"—a little child's hymn that they would like.

The doctor came in and pronounced her dead. They were getting Dorothy ready for her burial. And the little girls were running around in the living room, excited about Christmas, on the other side of the doors. And children were running upstairs.

My father and my mother told the older girls to go up and quiet the children upstairs, and try to explain to everyone, considering their ages, what had happened. So the older ones went upstairs. Years later I asked a sister, "Weren't you sad?" She said, "Of course, we all were sad. But my mother was very religious. And she prepared us, every step upon the way about how we might feel." She knew that when you're young, your feelings are just here one minute and gone the next. So she didn't expect little ones to sit down and weep and sob.

Because, it was Christmas Eve! And Santa Claus was coming! A week before that somebody had come to the door selling trees. And my older sister Helen said, "Oh, we have to have a tree." Mum said, "Oh, I don't know." Dorothy wasn't dead at the time, though she was languishing. These are old expressions that come to me: languishing. Sounds very Victorian, I think.

So they did have an uncooked turkey in the icebox and a bare tree in the living room—nothing on it. My mother had said, "I don't feel as if I want to bring out ornaments or things like that right now." That was before Dorothy died. She just didn't feel like it. She didn't have the spirit of Christmas.

My oldest sister Helen was possibly seventeen. My mother asked her to get the little ones ready for bed. And Mum and Dad and the minister were in with Dorothy.

But my older sisters said to one another, "You

know, this is not right. These kids are excited. What are we going to do?" And Helen said, "Look. I'll get the children ready for bed. We'll let them hang up their stockings." We had the stockings and Christmas decorations in boxes in the attic. They dug them out. They even had names on them.

So Helen said, "You leave it to me about putting the stockings up." But another sister said, "I don't know. Mum will think it's sacrilegious. It's not right to do this in the midst of death." So Viola went to Dad. She said something like, "Dad, this is a very sad day. But the little ones—they were waiting for Santa Claus. What can we do?" Dad said, "You leave it to me. I'll talk to your mother."

So he talked to Mum. No one knows what he said. But he must have said the right thing. Because she relented, and said that they could have Christmas, but they were to keep it low-key, and just remind the children that it is a festive season, but their sister had just died. That's a difficult thing to do. I would think almost impossible. You know, Santa Claus!

Helen said, "Okay. You two girls go, hurry. There's a turkey in the ice chest. I've got to start it." Helen cooked—she was the greatest cook. I think it was in her fingertips. And she prepared the turkey, while the other two went shopping for gifts.

They went to the stores, and as Viola said to me years later, "What a great thing! Everything was fifty percent off! The night before Christmas! We got so much stuff. We purchased gifts for everyone. Dad gave us what little money he had." They said, "Oh, we got even more than what we had hoped."

After my sisters left the stores: "We were bundled! We were coming down Chebucto Road towards Swaine Street, laden down with parcels, and laughing." And they looked around in the street. And our house was the only one dark, with the funeral crepe on the door.

They told me that they noticed the gloominess and the darkness in the wreath on our door. One of them said, "It struck me, the contrast. I was so happy. Then all of a sudden it came over me just what had happened, and why there was such a difference to the other houses."

All the other houses were lit up with wreaths on the doors and lights or candles in the windows.

When they got in the house, there was a smell of cooking. And there was a little low hum of the organ in the parlour, where the door was closed. It was getting late. And it was the old-fashioned coal stove, a large bird roasting in the oven. You could feel the heat as soon as you got in the house. And it was so cold outside.

"We assigned each other tasks." Helen was to finish decorating the tree, in between getting the turkey ready. Viola was to wrap the presents, and another sister was to fill the stockings. "We worked really, really fast." Boxes that Mum had stored away marked "Christmas" were all carried down into the living room. "We knew that the children would be up earlier, because it was Christmas."

It just worked out so well. In the midst of all their

sorrow—all this activity, this happy, festive occasion on one side of the sliding doors. And on the other side, there was organ music, and a child being prepared for burial. The minister coming and going. The soft organ music would stop occasionally as my mother knelt in prayer.

My father would come from the parlour every so often, and check to see what was going on in the living room.

I WAS EIGHT DAYS OLD. And we didn't leave that street until I was about seven years old. My brother and I would go outside and we'd look up at the moon. Sometimes there was a shadow, sometimes it was a full moon. Sometimes to my eyes the little shadow was like somebody sitting there. I'd say, "Oh, look, Jackie! Dorothy's looking!"

And Mum said Dorothy was watching over us. My mother was very spiritual. Even to this day I can see her. And I can still picture us then: "Jackie, look! Look! There's Dorothy!" He'd say, "Yeah. I think that's Dorothy." We'd come in and tell Mum we saw Dorothy. In the moon. And we'd always say, "Hi, Dorothy! Hi, Dorothy! Mum, I saw Dorothy!"

CHAPTER TWO

My Mother and Clark Gable

MY MOTHER WAS A WONDERFUL LADY. Born in 1889. Her father was a Baptist minister. When she was perhaps five years old her mother died. And that left her and her brother with her father, in the Baptist-type atmosphere. By that I mean: no cards. The music was just organ music from the church, and a few operas and things like that. No makeup. No parties. My mother told me this, and that was what she knew, or didn't know, of the outside world.

When she was in her early teens her father, the Reverend Henry Hatcher Johnson of Virginia, felt she needed a bit of polish to her whole being. She needed to become a real lady. So he sent her to the Boston Ladies Finishing School. And when she finished, at the end of that year, she came home. Her father was very pleased with her, with her whole being. At the college she learned a bit of music—what you call good music—and the art of writing—she had a beautiful

8

handwriting style, penmanship I guess you'd call it. I can see it to this day.

She learned entertaining, being a lady—not serving, but how to be served. Like being mistress of a household. So she came home and her father was very pleased. My mother was ready to reign in her father's home.

But a year or so later, when she was in her late teens, she met my father, James A. Davis. He was twenty; she was seventeen. And they fell in love, and they got married. She had fallen in love with the man of her dreams—if she had dreams, and I'm sure she did. When she married him, she settled down to a life of taking care of family. As most women did those days, you married, you took care of your family. Thick or thin, that's what you did.

Mum and Dad had a large family: fifteen children, eleven survived. They had nine girls. And she wanted to bring them up a little differently, with a little more freedom than she had. She didn't want to hold them that close, like she had been, but she still had her strict ways. You don't read what she'd call trashy, pulpy magazines. You don't have them in your home. You don't have cards in your home, playing cards.

You have girls growing up in different times, changing times, and you have one or two that might say, Well, I'll do what Mum says. There's always one or two who are going to be rebellious—not rebellious to the point that they answer back—we never did that at home—but rebellious to the point of—they might see a movie magazine. "Ooh, look at that!" They might even buy it. But they'd know they're not allowed to have it at home.

How many young girls or young boys have done something like that, brought something home they're not supposed to have? My sisters brought them home, and they would read the magazines—like *Photoplay*, I think it was called. And then they'd hide it under the mattress.

Now, I don't know what they thought Mum did, but she certainly stripped beds all the time, and she would find these magazines—she told me this later on—she would find the "trashy" magazines and say, "This is where this goes." And the magazine went in the trash.

What we didn't know was that Momma would retrieve them, and go to her room, when Dad was asleep or when we were out, whatever time she would get to herself. She would read, look over the magazines—these terrible magazines that we weren't allowed to see—which she should have seen if they had something like that when she was growing up, but she never did. Mum had never been to a movie in her life, never ever. She read about them.

That's how she saw this picture—and I saw the picture—of Clark Gable in one of the magazines. He was wearing a white turtleneck sweater. And he had that look. And when I tell that story I ask the audience, Is anyone here aware of Clark Gable, are you of that era? Hands go up. Well, I tell the younger ones that they will have to realize that Clark Gable was the king of Hollywood. He reigned in Hollywood in the '30s and the '40s. Women were wild about him. Why were they wild about him? Was it his muscular chest, was it his broad shoulders, was it his patent leather hair, was it that crooked smile he had—that deadly crooked smile—was it that neat mustache, or was it his ears? Because some women found those large ears cute.

I don't know what it was. But it was the combination perhaps of the whole thing that made Mum feel this way about that man. She'd never seen him, never seen the movies. So she was cutting out pictures that we didn't know about and putting them away, putting them away.

And then one day a good friend called. This is 1939. War had started in Europe. War was imminent, coming to Canada—the king and queen had been here, on a good fellowship trip, cementing Commonwealth ties—a good relationship tour. My mother went to Red Cross meetings. People were talking about having air raid practice, talking about using blackout curtains. It was getting to that point where it was a surety that we were going to be in it, we were getting our heels dug in, getting ready for war.

So maybe this is why Mum decided to go to the movies, for the first time in her life. Her friend Eva called her. The phone rings: "It's Eva, Gwen."

"What do you want, Eva?"

"You saw the newspaper, you saw the *Mail Star*?"

"Yes."

"Well, he's coming! You're going, aren't you?"

Mum said, "Well, I don't know, Eva."

"Oh come on, Gwen." Probably something like the "Lighten up!" of that day. "We're going, we're going—okay?"

Mum said, "Ahh, yes, I'll go."

So, they decide on what day.

So, the phone rings again. Eva says, "Gwen, did you see in the paper that the movie is so long, four hours, that they're having an intermission, they're having a place you can go to get a little snack?"

Mum said, "We're not going to buy anything. It'll cost us to get into the movie. We don't have that kind of money. We're taking our own lunch."

Eva says, "I'll bring the Big 8"—that was pop. "And the paper cups, and peppermints. What'll you bring, Gwen?"

"Well, let me see. I'll bring some napkins. I'll make some cookies, and I'll bring the sandwiches."

Eva says, "You're not making those egg sandwiches, are you?"

"Well, why not?"

Eva says, "Well, you know, in a closed area, they kind of smell."

And Mum said, "Oh, no no no. Okay, I'll bring ham and cheese."

"Good," she said, "now we're all settled as to what we're going to do."

The phone rings again the next day.

"What are you wearing?"

Mum said, "I never thought about what to wear."

Eva tells her, "I read somewhere that Clark Gable likes his ladies in blue."

My mother said, "Really? Oh, okay."

The day dawns. The big day. It is a Friday. They're going to see the matinee. Clark Gable in *Gone with the Wind* with Vivien Leigh. Mum gets dressed.

On her right cheek my mother had a strawberry birthmark, which when she was excited, upset or angry, the red marks would stand out on her cheek. They were standing out on this day. She was trying to act calm, but I could tell she was getting excited because she was going to a movie, and she was going to see Clark Gable.

Mum came down the stairs. Her friend Eva was at the door. Each of them looked each other up and down. My mother had on a black coat with dolman sleeves— wide in the arms and small at the wrists. Small hat. Her face was flushed. Her coat was slightly opened. And she had on a blue dress I'd never seen before. I said, "Mum, where did you get that blue dress?"

My mother looked at me. And when my mother gave me The Look, I stopped. I wasn't supposed to mention her dress. I stopped.

Eva had on a two-tone blue dress. My mother carried the bag. You could just see the top of the shoebox with her sandwiches and cookies in it. The box was tied with blue ribbon.

As they were going to go out the door, my father said, "Gwen, look, it's not a very nice day, it's drizzling and it may start raining. Perhaps I'd better give you ladies the money to get the taxi."

My mother firmly said, "No thank you, Jim. I have my own. We're taking the trolley. Thank you very much.

They got on the trolley and away they went. My father was standing there with a smile on his face.

So I got home from school. And my mother was there, she'd just come in. My dad was sitting in the easy chair by the coal stove in the kitchen. It was nice and cozy in there. And he was reading his paper. He was always reading. Mum had her apron on. But it looked like everything was done in a hurry. It looked like she'd tied the apron quickly and one of the strings had come undone, it was hanging down. It wasn't like my mother to wear an apron with the string hanging down. But I didn't say anything to her.

Mum said to me, "Get the table set early, Wanda, because we're having stew. I've got biscuits in the oven, and they should be out just about the time that Jackie gets home."

I said to her, "Mum, this movie you went to—*Gone with the Wind*—did you like it?"

"Oh yes, it was very nice."

"Mum, it was about the Civil War, wasn't it?"

"Yes," she said, "it's based on the American Civil War, with a story about the lives of families."

"Well, Mum, can I go? I should go to that because we have it in school, about the Civil War, and maybe I'd learn more about the war."

My mother kind of stiffened slightly and said, "Well—there's no need for you to go to that movie, because any information you want to know about the Civil War you can get at the library or in your school."

Anyway, we're there in the kitchen, and she's stirring the stew and the biscuits in the oven begin to smell kind of nice, and the room is warm.

The door flies open—and my brother jumps in, my brother Jackie—that scamp Jackie—jumps in and says, "Hi, folks, what's happening?" Throws his cap on the hall rack but it falls to the floor, and he jumps over it and he says, "Hi Pop, hi Sis. Hi Mum, I know where you've been."

And he comes in the kitchen, and—"Jackie, stop that." He's teasing. "Mum, come here, come here." And he's dancing around—that's what he did, anyway—dancing around the kitchen with his arm around Mum's waist. "Jackie, stop that, stop that." And her face is all flushed. "Stop that, Jackie, stop that. Go wash up. Supper'll be ready in about twenty minutes."

Jackie said, "Mum, tell me something. Hattie McDaniel was in that, wasn't she? What did you think about her?"

Mum said, "You know, I thought she was a very fine actress, very fine." She said, "Really, I'm not the one to ask, because this was my first movie. But," she said, "it was wonderful."

And she's stirring the pot. And she took the biscuits out of the oven.

Jackie said, "Mum, wait a minute. Wait a minute, Mum. What did you really think, when Clark Gable said that word, you know, Mum, that: 'Frankly, my dear, I don't give a damn.'"

My mother straightened up to her full five feet and looked directly at my brother—this was the first time she really looked at him since he came in—and she said slowly and distinctly, "Clark Gable had to say that. It was in the script. Clark Gable is a gentleman."

My father was behind his newspaper, trying not to burst out laughing. Jackie goes, "Pssshhhhhh." He just breaks out in this raucous laughter and flies down the hallway. And Mum went back to stirring the pot. But she was all flushed. She kept talking: "He *had* to say it." Because he was a gentleman. "And it was in the script." And a little later: "He was *supposed* to say it. He was paid to say that."

As though he could never say "damn" if it killed him. As much as to say that the director said, "Look, Clark, you've got to say 'damn.' Now, break all rules: say 'damn.'"

My poor mother. I never heard her say "damn," "hell," anything like that. But that was the story.

CHAPTER THREE

Mum Fights for Her Kids

WITH SO MANY CHILDREN came the joys and burdens of so many lives. Before I was born, my sister Hazel died. And at the same time, my sister Viola was very, very sick. She had pneumonia. Very ill. And the doctor said, "I don't hold out much hope for her."

In the meantime, Hazel was dying. And I think of the hardships of women at that time, who had so many children and not enough assets to support them, to take care of them. But our mother took care of us so well.

And Hazel died. And I don't know what she died of. The minister was there. They were saying prayers over Hazel's coffin. And Mum had to excuse herself, she said, because the doctor was with Viola.

Mum said, "I was praying for my dead child, and praying for the life of my other child."

Mum said that it was very hard, when a woman

17

is burying her daughter, a child, and she has to leave midway through the service to check on her other daughter who she thinks is also dying. That other daughter was Viola. Who lived.

WHEN MUM WAS NEEDED, when she *knew* she was needed, she never fell apart. When my brother Alan was diagnosed as schizophrenic, our doctor signed the papers that said he couldn't do any more with him, that he would have to commit Alan. Alan had been at home but was becoming unmanageable.

The hospital orderlies were outside, ready to take him. We were all standing around. My father began to cry, and the tears started to roll. Mum turned to him and said, "Jim. Be strong for the children. Not in front of the children, please. Be strong."

She was hurting as much as he was. But never a tear.

Mum went with Alan to the mental hospital in Dartmouth. And I went with Mum. Dr. Hopgood explained to my mother, "We're going to start a series of treatments on your son. And I would advise you not to come over. It'll be at least a month to six weeks, but we will let you know." And they gave her some tickets for the ferry, to come back and forth between Halifax and Dartmouth.

I think perhaps three weeks went by. My mother said, "I can't stand this any more. I have to see Alan. I'm going over." I went with her. The doctor said, "Oh, Mrs. Davis, I don't think you should see him today."

Mum said, "I'm seeing my son."

We saw him. My mother instantly knew that it had been a mistake to come. He had dropped a lot of weight. He was in a straitjacket. They had been giving him electric shock treatments. He didn't know us. His eyes looked wild. He was extremely agitated. And I was very young. I was afraid.

My mother said, "Now, Alan, this is Mum. This is Wanda." No response at all. We stayed about fifteen minutes, and we left.

She told the doctor, "It's not your fault. But I've seen him. I wanted to see him." And she said, "You'll let me know when I can come again."

We came home on the ferry. I'd look at my mother. She kept looking at one spot. When we got home, she went into her bedroom. I know she cried.

Then she came out and silently prepared supper.

I don't know why I get so emotional. That happened a long time ago. After that, Mum never missed a Sunday seeing him. Or, she brought him home on Sunday. She never missed his birthday. And when she was dying, she couldn't speak very well. She had cancer. And I was sitting by her bedside in the hospital. I was tired. I had a job then and I was looking after my boys and Dad at home. I was dozing in the chair by her bedside. Her hand came out and touched mine.

And she said, "Alan."

I said, "Mum, don't you worry. I'll never forget him. I can't be like you. But I will try to take your place."

And I did. Every Sunday. Every holiday, except

when I was away, I went to see him. I married Joe. He took me in the car; we took Alan on drives. He was moved to the new Abbey Lane Hospital. And he was still withdrawn. I took him his cigarettes, and his grapes—he liked grapes. And he called Joe "Pop."

One night he broke out. He jumped out the window. And he ran to where we had lived, on Swaine Street, halfway across the city. In his pyjamas. He loved it out there. There were fields behind our house where we picked berries.

The people that bought that house recognized him, and they called us, early in the morning. Dad went to get him and took him back to the hospital. Later, I saw my mother disappear again into the bedroom. Both my mother and my father.

ALAN NEVER GOT ANY BETTER. I don't know why I'm so emotional, because I don't mean to be. It happened a long time ago. I have other brothers who have died and I think of them. But not in the same way.

All my other brothers were older. And they wanted Alan to stay in school because they realized his potential.

And during the summer holidays one year my brother Gordon worked for Colwell Brothers. They were a men's clothing store, sort of an elite fashionable place downtown. And they offered him a two-week vacation, if he could find a reliable replacement. So Gordon said to Alan, "Here's two weeks you could work—and they'll pay you."

Alan wasn't a person that talked a lot. He was

seventeen. He just said, "I don't want to."

And of course, the girls in the family got after him saying, "You're selfish. Dad and Mum need the money."

So, reluctantly, he said he would go. Colwell's had clothing to deliver. Alan would walk to the houses in the South End. He was a delivery boy, and he also helped around the store, cleaning up and odd jobs—that sort of thing.

By the end of the week, he was taking so long to deliver parcels that it became a store joke. And one time, he was out delivering a parcel, going up the South End. And the next thing my mother got a call from the police. And it seemed that Alan had turned around and hit an older man in the face. Alan said, "He called me names. Called me names."

The gentleman did not press charges. He suggested to my parents that they take Alan to a doctor.

Alan was hearing voices then.

THAT IS HOW IT STARTED. That incident. Alan and my brother Jackie shared a bedroom. He would wake Jackie up at two or three in the morning, and say, "Look! Jackie. Jackie, wake up! There's signs! There's signs on the house!" He said the signs read: "Alan Davis is a coward."

And Jackie would go downstairs and go outside and look. And Jackie said, "There's no signs."

Alan was always quiet. He did very well in school. He played neighbourhood hockey and baseball with the boys on the Commons, and was in amateur boxing. And my older brother Harry was a porter on the railroad. And he would come in on his layover from Montreal. Montreal to Halifax runs. And he and Alan were good pals. When Alan was younger, Harry said, "I'm going to groom this guy. He could be a lightweight boxer."

So Alan had little matches in Truro and some other places close to Halifax. My mother always thought later, "He was punched in the head a lot. That's why there's something wrong."

So she had him tested. They said there's nothing wrong with him. So Mum wrote to Dr. Wilder Penfield, the famous neurosurgeon. My mother was writing letters all the time. If she read or heard about something she thought was politically, educationally or racially wrong, she would write letters to the newspapers, and to other people, expressing her opinion. They were all handwritten with this beautiful penmanship she was taught in the girls' school.

Anyway, she wrote out Alan's case, the whole story—all the details. And Dr. Penfield wrote back. He arranged for a thorough examination. Alan was diagnosed with dementia praecox. This is called schizophrenia today. My mother was devastated.

Meanwhile, Alan was getting worse. He wouldn't sleep. He'd sleep in the day, be up all night. The whole household was turned upside down. And they told us he would have to be hospitalized. I think Mum never got over that. But I don't want to put it that way. It sounds so inane—"She never got over that." She was very strong in her faith. And when she questioned why, she would just go to her room, and I think she prayed. She prayed. And she never forgot Alan.

So, we were there at the hospital—every Sunday. Alan would sit there quietly. He wasn't bad, but he wasn't good. They wanted to get him engaged in something, crafts or in the kitchen. They'd find him in a corner doing nothing. He didn't interact with anybody.

At that time, Viola was working, building her beauty care business. She would come to the house on Sunday sometimes, we'd have dinner. And one time, before Alan was taken away—Alan had never danced; he never did anything like that—but this Sunday there was a record playing. And Alan jumped up. And he grabbed Viola. And he started to dance and dance, and he wouldn't stop dancing. And Viola said, "Well, it doesn't matter. It doesn't matter." My brother Gordon said, "He's got to stop!" Viola said, "Let him dance."

I don't know how long it was, but the music kept going and Alan kept dancing and dancing—even after the music stopped. Finally my brother Gordon went over and put his hand on Alan's shoulder. Alan turned and roughly shoved Gordon away. He stopped a little while after that, and curled up on the couch and went to sleep.

So this was before he was hospitalized. He had to be put away. Night was day and day was night. And he was hallucinating.

VIOLA NEVER FORGOT HIM. She'd be working, and she would get something for him, for Mum to take out.

She never came out to the hospital, no. But when we brought him home, she always came to the house. We had dinner together. And she would talk to him. He would occasionally turn, stare briefly at Viola, and then go back to his world. I would talk to Alan, then I stopped. Because he never answered.

And when Viola died in 1965, she left money for his care, anything he would need.

I LOVED ALAN. He loved animals. He was a very kind person. And you could feel it. Even though he was quiet, you could feel that he was part of the family. My brother Jackie—fun-loving little rascal. And my brother Harry—I worshipped him. He was so kind and so nice and loved his sisters. Would do anything for us. He was fiercely protective of his sisters. Always. Even up until he died.

Alan came home this Sunday—we brought him home. And Viola was saying, "Alan, you remember So-and-so." Trying to draw him in. I was very young then. He looked around. And he stopped eating. He looked at me. "Wanda," he says, "the good-looking girl." I was maybe fourteen or fifteen. And Viola says, "Ho ho ho! Alan, you want to look again?" Something like that, trying to make light of it. And then he went off into his own world. His eyes were so intense, so dark.

And when I married Joe, we used to take Alan out in the car. And we had little Joey. And Alan would sit in the visiting room and watch Joey. A little smile, every now and then.

But the very last Sunday, it was snowing. Joe and

I went over. Alan didn't want to come home for dinner. We took him his cigarettes, and some grapes. He took a cigarette, started to smoke. His fingers were all gone yellow. And Joey was running around—a year and a half.

And Alan got up abruptly. He grabbed his bag, and he went out. And he liked Joe and me, he did. He never said he liked him, but you could tell he was comfortable with Joe. When he married me, Joe took on the family, too. He helped with my boys, and with Alan. I don't know why anybody would be that brave or foolish, in 1971, to marry a divorced woman of a different race, with three young boys and a schizophrenic brother, but he did.

We were home. The phone rang. Alan had had a heart attack. And he was taken to the hospital. "Should I come?" "Oh no no no no no. They're stabilizing him now."

Anyway, I was working. And Joe called, picked me up, and we went to the Victoria General Hospital. When we got there, you could see in the distance they were working over Alan. And they came out, and they told me that he had gone, there was nothing they could do for him.

And I lost him, again. When I got home, like my mother, I went to my room, closed my door—and I bawled and bawled and bawled.

CHAPTER FOUR

Music in Our Home

WHEN I THINK OF MY CHILDHOOD HOME I think of it as a happy home, a warm home with the smell of Mum's cooking—and with music. Music throughout the house.

I want to capture the atmosphere of the house, because there was music everywhere—music all the time. Everybody had their own favourites.

My oldest brother Harry had a tenor voice. He loved semi-classic. He sang in the church choir at Cornwallis Street Baptist Church. He loved Yusi Bjorling and Enrico Caruso. And Harry liked John McCormack—the Irish songs and also the parlour songs, like "I'll See You Again." He had a light tenor—he would sing so sweetly—you could hear him in his room. He'd be getting his shoes polished, getting ready to go to work, with his cap and uniform.

He had become a chauffeur for Mr. Dennis, William H. Dennis, the newspaperman who owned the

Chronicle Herald. He was fortunate to find work.

The Depression was a terrible blow for our family. Both my mother and father were very upset because they had to take Harry out of school. You know, everybody was doing it. Dad was working intermittently, had a little bit here and there. It wasn't enough. So my brother Harry—he was a prince. A king. My brother loved everybody. And he took over. I think during those days young men had to step up to the plate and help, when they had a big family like we did.

And Harry always encouraged us to study. He stood over us, doing our homework. He always wanted to know what we were doing. And when he went away, he always called Mum, checking what was going on. He was so family-oriented.

And Harry sang all the time.

The whole house was music. When I would come in at lunch hour, my mother would have the radio on. That wasn't all music. She would have Anna Dexter on CHNS, household tips, hints, something like Heloise today. Then after that, she would listen to Julius Silverman who would play violin, which she loved. In the afternoons she had the "soaps"—*Pepper Young's Family* or *One Man's Family*. In the background Dad would put on a record. Mum'd be getting supper ready. Harry would come in, "Can I change that?" And he'd put on his music.

When TV came in, Mum and Dad would clear the decks for *Don Messer's Jubilee*. And they loved Juliette—"Our Pet." And Tommy Hunter.

It was like a circus! We only had the one gramophone. But we had piles of records. The older sisters, they liked the foxtrot and the music of the day.

My Uncle Jack, Dad's brother, came in for dinner sometimes. He also sang in the church choir, he had a tenor voice. His was heavier than Harry's, very, very nice. He formed a quartet in Halifax—The Halco Quartet. "That Gal of Mine" type of song or "Boy of Mine" or "Because." There were some religious. Not the hallelujah-type religious. My uncle would sing "The Lord's Prayer." He was not a gospel singer.

"Will Your Anchor Hold?" My father loved that Anglican hymn. "When Day Is Done" and "What Is My Reason for Living"—parlour songs!

That was really part of everybody in our household. Everybody. My brother Jackie, the youngest boy, he thrived on music. He loved to sing the love songs that were popular then. He had a voice, if he'd been born around today, he'd be on *American Idol*!

We were always singing. My sisters sang together in the house, the four of them, and they'd sing in harmony. Really, really nice. It wouldn't be Helen because by the time I remember anything, Helen was married. I know Olive and Viola were part of it. The four would sing together, songs of the day—the songs of the 1930s and '40s mostly.

They really liked the uplifting songs—not gospel but "I love you a bushel and a peck." And the love songs of the Ink Spots or Mills Brothers or Nat King Cole.

They'd gather around to sing. By the time the '40s came, that old gang was breaking up! Because one went to Montreal, and Viola was working, started her beauty shop. But when it was happening, it wasn't rare. We were singing all the time. It would be spontaneous. One would start to sing in the kitchen, doing dishes. And the other one would be joining in. Suddenly we'd all be together singing. It was two or three times a week. Maybe more.

I love to sing, any time, any place. I don't say I sing well, I just love to sing and listen to singers. I sang on the radio. There was a program called *Uncle Mel's Children's Hour*. And Uncle Mel was Mr. Hugh Mills from Mills Brothers, a fashionable ladies' clothing store on Spring Garden Road. My brother Harry took me to the radio station. I auditioned, and they put me on!

It was so pleasant coming home, after school. The sisters would be singing. Harry would be in his room humming. Or you'd hear him in the bathroom, singing "I'll See You Again."

My father was not a singer. His brother Jack was a great singer. But my father—he loved "Will Your Anchor Hold?" And on Sundays that was his contribution. Mum would come in on the last line in a trembly voice, "Grounded firm and deep in the Saviour's love."

Dad sang it with such fervour that it made up for lack of tone. And we were okay with it, because he didn't sing anything else! Once in a while he'd sing an Anglican hymn.

My mum loved the gospel-type—the Baptist hymns. She had a very soft voice, and she would sing. In our home Mum was famous for "Rock of Ages." And "Abide with Me." When I went with her to church, she would sit there and listen to the choir singing a Baptist hymn, and she just loved it. Loved it.

And she used to sing Baptist hymns in a very quiet little voice in the kitchen. Every now and then when she was cooking, you'd hear them.

On Good Friday, we'd all get ready and go to the long afternoon service at the Anglican church. Mum would come with us. Before she left, she would start her hot cross buns. With yeast. And come with us. Then, a little while into the service, she would quietly leave church and go home to get the rolls ready for the next stage. Then she'd come back to church, just before service was over. I'm sure she asked God's forgiveness.

When everybody arrived home, you could smell the hot cross buns—and Dad would say, "They're ready, Gwen. They're risen and ready for the oven!" I remember putting the icing cross on them. Hot cross buns!

But that is the only time I remember her going to the Anglican church.

THERE WAS NOTHING IN OUR RELIGION that forbade singing almost any kind of song that the family wanted to sing. Even popular songs—my mother did not object to anything like that. When I came home from the States, my father and mother had their Elvis records. They both loved Elvis. Mum liked his religious songs. Dad liked the rock-and-roll.

Although Mum never danced herself, she permitted dancing in our home.

Helen moved back into our house on Swaine

Street with her husband. They had the downstairs, before they bought a house or got an apartment. And they didn't have any children yet. And they were fun-loving people. I mean, she was nineteen or twenty and she loved parties, she loved singing, she loved dancing. Helen was the sprite of the family, the comedian. She was amazing. She was always up!

She said she was going to have a party—any old excuse for a party. Husband Bert was coming home that day, so they were having a party. So I was there. I was about three. My brother Jackie was two years older. We watched the adults dancing. We were supposed to be in bed. We watched through the posts on the stairs. They would roll back the rug, wind up the Victrola, and Harry would stack up the records. And the girls would come—my sisters and their friends. And older people.

Because it wasn't just a young person's party. Those days, all ages were there. Older people, your aunties and your uncles and your grandmums—they were all there at the party. Everybody was having a good time. Mum went in the kitchen and got things ready for the little repast, as they called it—little snack.

Dad never danced or anything like that, but he listened and joined in the banter. He always had his newspaper somewhere in a corner. He never danced. And my mother didn't dance because Baptists didn't dance.

EXCEPT ONCE. Mum told me one time she *did* dance. One time. She said, "It was like floating on air."

It happened like this:

My mother was graduating from the Boston Ladies Finishing School. She told me that her father, Rev. Johnson, had a man working for him, a bookkeeper. She went to her father and she asked for a new dress—for the dance, for the school's graduation festivities. Her father said to her, "Gwendolyn"—you have to imagine a very lanquid southern accent—"Gwendolyn. I think I gave you a beautiful dress when you started college. Now that will be sufficient for you to wear at your graduation. I paid a lot of money for that dress."

Mum told me that she told the bookkeeper and he said, "Miss Johnson. Miss Johnson. I'll talk to your father, and maybe, maybe he'll change his mind."

He must have, because she was given the money to buy a new dress or to have one made. And she told me that she went to the dance. My mother told me she wore a beautiful blue gown but she was not supposed to dance.

She told me, "I had the time of my life." She said, "I danced a waltz." She said, "I can't even remember the boy's face, because my eyes were closed." She said, "I danced as if I was on air. I just enjoyed it. It was so beautiful. I never missed a step. I just felt like I was floating. And I had a new dress on. And I was dancing, for the first time."

The girls must have been taught dancing in school, how to do a little step or waltz or whatever. Mum didn't learn it at home. She didn't have a mother.

And I have to sort of piece it together. I never thought

about it quite like this before. She said, "I danced."

And she never danced again. My father never danced. Mum never danced. She never went to movies except that once.

"But," she said, "I'll never forget it, as long as I live. I had this beautiful dress on. I never opened my eyes. I was in tune—I never missed a step. I loved it. It was a waltz."

And that's true. She told me because by then she had a little more time, to talk to me, being the youngest. She told me she danced once and never again.

BUT ANYWAY, YEARS LATER, in her own home, Mum's children were allowed to roll up the rug, get the Victrola going and dance. I don't know what they had for drinks. There was a big punch bowl. But they wouldn't serve liquor if Mum was there, and Mum was there. There was a window seat. People were sitting there. And the girls had flapper-type dresses—colourful, colourful dresses.

Many were smoking. My father smoked all the time. And the music—after all this time—I still hear strains of some of those tunes.

And the two of us kids were on the stairs. My sister said, "Look at Wanda and Jackie. It's late. I'll put them back to bed." And Mum said, "Oh, let them stay. Let them listen to the music for a little while. I'll see they get to bed." And we sat there thinking nobody saw us. They were dancing the Charleston. And one of the songs was "The Peanut Vendor."

That was early Depression time. But, of course,

wherever Helen was, nobody was depressed. Her husband had a steady job. I'm not saying that she was inane, or laughing at everything. But Burt had a job with CN. And he brought in a pay cheque.

My father had only intermittent work. He didn't work steadily. My brother Harry worked every day. Everybody else was in school. Viola would have been in her last years of high school.

A lot of mouths to feed in that house. But I can't remember going hungry. I'm sure Mum did her best. But I remember Viola telling me years later, when I was in trouble in the United States, "If you are your mother's daughter, you know how to stretch food." Viola was there trying to help me learn how to stretch my very few dollars.

During the Great Depression, I was very young, but still I don't feel I grew up feeling deprived. My parents had a talent for not making us feel those things. Mum, particularly, being a great mother.

And I remember one time—it must have been an especially hard time. There were tears in Mum's eyes. We were having supper. She turned around from the stove, and she put our plates on the table. My brother said, "We had this for breakfast!" My father looked at him. "Eat your supper."

Mum started to apologize. Dad said, "Don't—"

Mum said, "This is what we have tonight. This is all we have. We're all going to have the same thing, so nobody's getting any better or any worse."

So she sat down to her bowl of cereal. And I think we also had toast. And that was it.

CHAPTER FIVE

Introducing Viola

MY SISTER VIOLA was always immaculate. Chic and well coifed. She always seemed like she was monitoring her siblings, how you dressed, how you spoke. Even today, if I put a few "had"s in a sentence which aren't right, I correct myself. I feel her presence.

Viola was topnotch in school, all through school. She was quiet, she listened well, and she absorbed a lot. Perhaps because with her, everything had to be correct.

In the early '30s, Halifax schools did not hire black teachers, and the schools were segregated. The school system wanted to keep the blacks in Hammonds Plains, Preston, and in Africville, to be taught in their home areas. If you were black and going into Grade 12 and wanted to be a teacher, you could take a test to attain a special certificate which allowed you to teach in the black schools—a kind of dispensation. Viola attained one of these certificates. Viola taught at the Preston school and at Hammonds Plains.

Viola had students who were all ages and all

grades. And they were boys, often men, and girls—all different ages. Some of them had never been to school, and some of them had stopped and started again.

One day the superintendent of the schools visited. Viola was in her room teaching. The superintendent asked her to step outside of the classroom; he wanted to speak to her about her students. And she was telling him something about what she was teaching, and how many children she had, the age differences.

When she started to go back in, he said, "We've been out here about ten minutes. And you've got a class of children and semi-adults in there—and I haven't heard one sound out of that room."

"And," Viola said, "I don't think you will, either."

And she was just sixteen years old. And he remarked to the principal about how well-behaved her class was.

AND AS I UNDERSTAND IT, while she was studying in Grade 12, Viola read an article about Madam C. J. Walker, America's first self-made female multi-millionaire. Born in Louisiana, the woman who would become Madam C. J. Walker worked in the fields beside her parents, former slaves who were sharecroppers. They both died before she was eight years old. As a child, she went out with her father scrubbing and cleaning houses. She moved in with an older sister in Mississippi and she married at age fourteen to get away from the cruelty of her sister's husband. She had very little education. Her daughter Lelia was born in 1885. Her husband died two years later and Madam Walker moved to Missouri. She worked as a domestic and through her hard work she saw her daughter graduate from public schools and attend a black private college.

Madam Walker had some kind of a skin condition, or scalp condition, I believe. Her hair was falling out. She tried many products but none worked. So what she did was, she mixed up some oils and other things, and put them on her scalp, and she found that it worked well. In her book she says she had a dream about a mixture that would save her hair. Some of the mixture came from Africa. She made it and tried it. She experimented on herself, family and friends. And when she would go to work in other people's houses, they would come to her and say, "Could I have some of that?"

She realized that there were almost no hair products available for blacks. She decided to go into business, selling hair and scalp and skin products to black women. She sold her products door-to-door. And that's how she started her own business.

Her name wasn't Walker then. Eventually she married Charles Joseph Walker, a Denver newspaperman. He helped her with advertising and she developed a mail order business, establishing the C. J. Walker Manufacturing Company. It became an empire.

I am amazed, every time I read about it. I can't believe that one woman could do that. Black. Uneducated. And she made a lot of money. She was a leading black philanthropist, promoted black education, especially for women.

And Viola read about Madam Walker. And she was inspired. This woman's success is what got Viola going. She studied how Madam Walker started her own business. She started a school—the Madam C. J. Walker School of Beauty Culture. She trained girls for hair and skin—for black beauty. And all these girls went back to their homes, to their towns, and took that training there. Took the products. So Madam Walker had established a franchise. They were Madam C. J. Walker's girls.

And she built a mansion on the Hudson River. I can't believe it. I've seen photographs. And outside of the home are all these women she had trained, women who went out as her sales force and students all over the States. She had a swimming pool. It was a magnificent place. And this is in the early twentieth century—a hundred years ago.

And Madam Walker established the Lelia College in Pittsburgh, Pennsylvania. And then her daughter Lelia set up a second beauty school in New York.

Now, Viola wanted to study at that school, in New York, and that's where she eventually went. But Viola first studied beauty culture at a place in Montreal—the Field Beauty Culture School. She also earned a diploma from Madam Sara Spencer Washington's Apex College of Beauty Culture and Hairdressing in Atlantic City in 1940, and then a certificate from the Advanced Hairstyling Studio in New York in 1941. When Viola studied in New York, that certificate refers to her as "Miss." Not because she was hiding the fact that she was married, but because she wanted to stay at the YWCA. And at that time you could only stay there if you were a single woman.

So Viola saw the success of Madam C. J. and she said, "I want to do that. I want to do that." I understand her friend and schoolmate, the singer Portia White, encouraged her. Portia said, "Well, go ahead and do it."

So Viola taught school, and she saved her money, so she could go to Montreal and then to New York.

And her first trip to New York, she went by bus. She'd already had a year of training in Montreal and won a silver cup for her work. I was a little girl but I remember. They sat up, Mum and her, the night before, getting ready for her to go to the big bad city. Viola had some money. Mum said, "I don't think you should carry it in your purse."

Mum sewed the money into Viola's bra!

IN NEW YORK, Viola studied beauty culture by day. At night, she worked at a nightclub called Small's Paradise. I'm sure she told our parents that she worked as a waitress. But I know that she was one of those "cigars-cigarettes" girls in the nightclub.

Viola said that she made more on tips than wages because the wages were very low.

She was serious about her studies. But she also had to eat. She may have told Mum and Dad she was waitressing, but she showed me the costume she wore. "Don't you ever tell Mum or Dad how small it was!"

It seemed like Hallowe'en, an orangey-yellow with black. It had little frills top and bottom.

She was so focused. She worked and studied. She did that for a couple of years, and then came back to Halifax. At that time our family had two apartments. For the first beauty shop she opened, she took over the first apartment. She and her husband Jack Desmond. He was a barber and she was a beautician. She did that for all the time she was studying, and coming back and forth to Montreal and to New York. And she subsidized her schooling by her work as a beautician in Halifax, and her part-time work where she studied.

In those days, there wasn't a black woman working in a professional beauty shop in Halifax. Nobody. If you went to a beauty parlour and you were black— well, you couldn't go. You'd be refused. I was refused in one shop in the 1970s. "We don't do you people's hair." Training facilities in Halifax restricted black women from admission.

Viola started her business. And, believe me, it was long overdue. And the women came to her. Women are human beings, whether they are black or white—they are women. They want to look good, they want to go out to a party. Viola did hair for the girls going to the proms, dances, even funerals. Viola's sister-in-law died, and she did her hair. Her best friend's mother died. She did her hair. That work was always gratis.

So, that's what Viola started. Then she left our family home to open her own shop. She bought a little shop around the corner on Gottingen Street, about four doors away. Viola Desmond's Beauty Store. She put her name on the windows, and she would later put her name on her products—just like Madam C. J. Walker. And eventually she had a girl working with her—Rose Gannon, a girl she could trust. She had trained Rose and Rose did exactly as Viola wanted, and she was, you know, reliable and hardworking. And the business grew.

Viola made face powders. She would get powder in bags, and mix them to make different shades. She called them by different names. She also made hair pomade.

Some of her clients asked her about other problems—people with black hair that doesn't grow, or it breaks off, or it's very hard to manage. So Viola decided, "I'm going to go back to school. I'm going to learn how to make wigs."

She left Rose Gannon to run the beauty parlour. My mother came in to help when she could. And Viola went back to New York and took a course in making wigs.

So Viola made hairpieces, falls, chignons and wigs. That is a very painstaking process; it takes a long time. But I'll tell you: Viola was well-paid for her work. Because her work was exemplary. You knew if she did something—if she was in the middle and she did something wrong—you wouldn't get it. She would go all over it again.

She taught my mother how to make wigs. So my mother had a good sit-down job.

And I worked for Viola too—fifty cents a week. I filled up the cans of pomade. Viola's picture—the picture we see everywhere today—was on the label. I put those on the cans.

She bought everything from the United States. I was working at the Fisheries Research by then and I would pick up her supplies from the Customs. She bought a set of scales, so you could weigh everything. She said, "If you're going to weigh for me, that scale has got to be accurate. And *you* have to be precise. I don't shortchange my customers."

She would check everything. Painstakingly. Boxes and boxes.

And during the war, she had many more customers. She worked full days, six days a week. Sundays she went with her husband to Dartmouth to Ocean View Manor, a senior citizens' home. Jack's mother was there. Jack's mother loved Viola.

BUT I DON'T WANT PEOPLE TO THINK that Viola was perfect. I'll let you in on a little secret. Viola said I was never to tell anybody!

Viola came to visit me in the States, and she said, "What are we having for breakfast?"

I said, "What would you like?"

"Oh," she said, "how about eggs? I love them poached. Poached on toast."

"Poached on toast it is!"

So, I gave her two eggs, on toast, two pieces of toast, and a cup of tea, and juice. Viola was almost smacking her lips—it's so vivid to me. It was so rare, because she would occasionally do the things that Mum wouldn't let us do. She ate the eggs quickly and she said, "Ah, that was good, Wannie. Do you think you could make me two more?"

Made her two more.

My boys went out to play in the back yard. Viola and I were talking. And she was scraping off her plate with a piece of toast. You could do all those things now—the children weren't there!

So I said, "Okay." I started to clear off the table. We were talking about old times. And she said, "Could I have another two eggs?"

That's six! That's six eggs! She said, "Don't you ever ever tell anybody I ate six eggs at your house at one sitting!"

Because it sounds greedy. It wasn't in character with Viola, who was a lady. People eat daintily. And when you finish, you use your napkin—this is what our mother taught.

But this was something rare, because Viola just about starved herself. I don't think it was to keep her figure, although she was short and did not want to be overweight. It was more that she had created a pattern of living—get up in the morning, and get to work, and get going. She was so driven. Sometimes she would forego lunch or forego anything to eat. I wouldn't say she starved herself deliberately. But she became very hungry. She learned to live this way, not eating for a long period, and then filling up. But she loved to eat.

She would drop in at our place, right on the corner, and eat at any time. At Mum's. And sometimes Mum would take her something. And if Mum was going to help her at the beauty salon—if Viola was overwhelmed with work—Mum would go in and she'd take her sandwiches or something.

But Viola didn't like to eat and work. That type of work—handling people's hair. You'd have to wash your hands and go sit down somewhere to eat. That meant she'd have to stop, and she didn't want to do that.

Being there for her customers came first, and second or third was herself. So the habit was there, not to eat. Not taking care of herself.

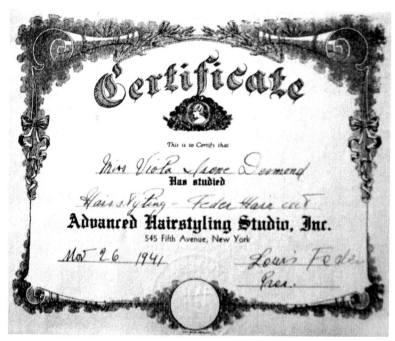

One of several diplomas Viola Desmond earned.

CHAPTER SIX

My Parents Were a Team

IKNOW THAT MY MOTHER loved my father, and my father loved my mother. You could feel the love in our home, especially during the Depression years. I'm not waxing poetic—nor did I wear blinders. I never felt like we children were a burden to them. We never felt like we couldn't say, "I need something." We'd ask, and they would try to get it, especially for school. They stressed, stressed, stressed education—both of them—education, education. If I asked my father for a word—"What does this mean?"—we lived with books, just like a library. My father would say, "I know what it is, now you go look it up and *you'll* know. Because if I tell you, you won't remember."

But should I tie myself to a vision of my mother's face disapproving? Because she would disapprove of elbows on the table! I mean, you couldn't reach across the table, you couldn't snuffle with your nose. You had your handkerchief. You had your napkin, always. Both Mum and Dad always monitored our table manners.

One of my children was about eight, when they were at the Halifax Grammar School and we were living with my parents. Gordon said, "Grandad, you know what? This boy, he took a book and he flinged it."

And everybody just froze—everybody did. You said flinged it? My other kids were there, looking—Thank god it's not me. Flinged it. My father stiffened. "I beg your pardon?" "Grandad?" He said, "Flinged it? F-f-flunged it? F-f-flanged it?" My father rolled his eyes. "Oh, Grandad," Gordon wailed, "I don't know!"

You just had to laugh.

MUM AND DAD WERE TOGETHER on the raising of the children. I'm not saying harmony. You had a younger crew and the older children. Eleven children in all. They had to establish rules.

Viola would be the youngest of the four oldest sisters. She was given the lighter duties because she was so tiny, and she had a tiny voice, and she was always reading. And my parents said she was delicate. But I'm told that really she was a tough little rascal. She was determined. Even as a little girl.

When Viola was small, the older kids went to Joseph Howe School. My father used to say to them, whenever they left the house, to watch out for Viola. She was very young, very little. I wasn't even born, but I'm told that they would each have to take her arm, because Viola would be afraid to walk through a puddle, if there was a little bit of water. My father and mother said to them every day, "Take care of Viola, you know she's delicate. So, don't you leave her behind. Because she walks slowly."

The others always felt that Viola was using this smallness as a gimmick. Harry was so good, so kind, he loved his sisters, but even he got a little exasperated with her.

And I understand she got to be a pain in the neck. She may have played on it, because it got to the point where, if there was grass, she wouldn't walk in it. There was something in the grass. So they'd have to pick her up by the arms and carry her over the grass.

BUT THEY WERE FAMILY. And when they came home, Viola had the job of putting away the dishes. She wouldn't *wash* the dishes but she'd put them away. And she had to set the table, and she had to clear everything off. But she never or very seldom washed any dishes.

And Viola never did any cooking, at all. The only thing she cooked was the icing on a cake, because she liked to do it, and she liked to eat it, and we liked to lick the beater.

Helen always baked. She was a superb cook. Viola seldom baked. But she had one specialty: Seven-Minute Frosting. Boiled Icing. If today you make it, it's no big deal with an electric beater. But then women were known for that skill. I'm talking about older women. Viola would put the ingredients in a double boiler. Water in the bottom. And you put your eggs and other ingredients in the top. And you take the hand beater and you beat it for seven minutes. That's why it's called Seven-Minute Boiled Icing. Viola would stand there, and she would beat beat beat beat. It was delicious!

And it was hard work. The women might spell each other—timing, timing. The icing was cooked on top of the stove, a coal and wood stove. And they would beat and beat. Helen would make the cake. She could have sold one to the queen.

But Viola—that icing was her specialty.

She helped Mum. Viola would have her own little footstool to get up and get dishes and put them on the back of the stove to warm the plates up before serving.

The others used to get kind of mad because Viola always got the easy jobs. But setting the table, she'd be careful with the silverware. Everybody else was pounding them on the table. And after the meal, she would scrape the plates, and she was finished! That was Viola.

She amazed me, because I never saw her do anything domestic. Her husband Jack did most of the cooking and cleaning. He didn't seem to mind.

Growing up, she always had her hands done up—doing her nails or something—or she was in the rocking chair reading. Of course the feeling was she's putting one over on them. It's her turn to do it, and she can't do it. In any case, the older girls did the bulk of the work, helping Mum.

Sunday night or early Monday morning, Mum

would strip the beds and soak the sheets. There were double sinks—set tubs—in the basement, and she would put bluing in one sink, and the white things in there, and the other sink was for rinsing. She didn't have a machine. So the girls would go down, before they went to school on a Monday morning, and they would have to help Mum put in the sheets, the bedding. Or if they soaked overnight or a few hours in bluing, making them white, Mum would start wringing them out. Mum did scrubbing. And the girls would hang out the sheets and pillowcases before leaving for school. And Mum would work on diapers and that after they'd gone.

My older sisters always helped with the younger ones. Changing diapers before they went to school, and getting them set up for their meal, the little ones.

The first thing when they came home, one would take one child, one would have the other. Their first job was to start changing diapers. Or else one would bring in the laundry if Mum hadn't already brought it in. Sometimes if it looked like rain, Mum would bring it in. Or one would bring it in and one would take a child and change it. We weren't the only family to have to do this, but we had a lot of children.

Gordon and Harry helped Dad by bringing in coal for the stove and taking out the ashes. Alan took out the garbage. When we had a dog it was Gordon's job to take him out, feed him and wash him.

My mother sent me handmade diapers for my first child in 1951. Handmade, hand-stitched diapers. And they lasted through all my children.

AND ONE TIME WHEN MY SISTER WAS SICK, very sick, and needed a lot of care, sometimes I'd come home early from school to help Mum with her. And she had to be hospitalized. Mum was with her a lot, and the older girls worked. And they learned how to cook a meal. Helped Mum in the kitchen.

I started school early because of that sister. She had never been able to attend school because of an illness. And she was shy. She'd been in the hospital a lot. She would have been eight in December. The doctor said, "Well, she should be going to Grade One." And he said, "You know, it would be nice if you could send that little one over there with her, her sister." That was me. He said, "You could ask the school, could she just be in the room with her sister, so her sister would feel comfortable, looking around and seeing her." And the school said, "Yes."

I was five when we went to Sir Charles Tupper School.

But of course, I wasn't going to just sit there. Even at home, I looked at everybody doing homework after supper. I was looking and peering, gathering—what I could understand, at my age. So when my older sister went into Grade One, I started too. I asked Mum could I have pencils and paper. So I did the work. The school said, "There's no reason why she can't go to second grade, with her sister." So I went into the second grade. And I went on to the third grade.

I MENTIONED BEFORE, we lived in a house on Swaine Street where I was born. We had a very large kitchen. And two steps down, there was a pantry. But my mother turned the pantry into a second kitchen, a small kitchenette. We had a table there, and the four younger children ate there. And one of the older daughters sat there to help serve and to help feed these younger ones, to make sure they ate.

Then you'd go up two steps and I can still see the big table. Everybody is there—Dad, brothers Gordon and Harry and Alan, and my sister Olive. Olive would be at the big table with my other sisters. They were all there. Homemade biscuits, buns, bread—whatever we had that day. And my mother would be looking over to the little kitchen to see how we little ones were getting on with either Helen or Viola. The older sister would usually be Helen.

And that's one way it comes back to me, the family together.

CHAPTER SEVEN

In the Halifax Explosion

MY OLDEST SISTER HELEN was the favourite of my grandmother—Dad's mother—Robena Davis.

Grandma Davis thought Helen was the bee's knees. Helen looked like her, too.

Mum and Dad were living with Dad's parents at that time, and Mum would chastise Helen, because Helen was precocious, talked early, walked early. In a house full of adults, this can happen. So she said she wanted to give Helen a spanking. And her mother-in-law Robena said, "Don't you touch that little girl. Don't you dare touch her."

Helen used to dress up and make up to copy her grandmother. Mum said you had to see it to believe it. She used to put on her grandmother's hat and dress and hike it up, her purse on her arm, and her shoes.

"Where are you going, Helen?"

"I'm going to the store," she said. "I'm going to buy something."

"Sorry, Helen. You can't go out alone."

Helen, stamping her foot, "I *must* buy groceries. The cupboard is empty!"

Mum said Helen was ruined by the time she got out of there.

WHEN I WAS BORN, Grandma Davis had been dead a few years. I don't know much about her. But the family tells a story about Grandma and the Halifax Explosion.

And my father told me that story. It is a very telling part of Mum and Dad's life, the Halifax Explosion in December 1917.

Now, I'm going to go back just a little bit. Early in 1917, Mum's father Rev. Johnson died in New Haven, Connecticut. She could not go to the funeral because she was either just going to give birth or had just given birth to my brother Gordon.

When she couldn't go to the States when her father died, she told her brother, "I'll be there later on." Well, a short time later, her brother died of a heart attack. He was only thirty-one. And her father was fifty-two when he died.

Anyway, it was less than a year—it was in late 1917—that her brother died in New Haven. The same year as her father. Now she had a small child. She decided she was going to go to her brother's funeral, because there was no one there for her father's things, nobody there to take care of anything. Her father—according to Mum—he had an antique business. Along with being a minister, he collected antiques and curios and paintings.

Mum said to Dad, "I must go." They were living on Gottingen Street. They didn't own the house, they rented it from this lady. They had the upstairs part, and she had the downstairs. She was a friend of my mom's, Mrs. Halfkenny.

Mum decided, "I have to go to New Haven." Dad said, "You leave the girls with me." There were four girls then. Viola was the youngest.

She went by train. Mum took the baby with her, the baby was Gordon. And she took the oldest boy with her, Harry, because all the older children always knew how to help with the younger ones. Even the boys—especially Harry.

She boarded the train in Halifax. Dad told me this. My sister told me too. My mother got as far as Truro. She's got a baby and the oldest son. She's on the way to her brother's funeral. And the train was stopped in Truro. Explosion in Halifax. Two boats collided in the harbour. You could feel it—you knew something happened—as far away as Truro. They stopped all the trains because they wanted the tracks open, for the emergency trains coming from Upper Canada and the United States, to bring medical supplies, doctors, nurses.

So they stopped her train. Mum got out, with her children.

Mum told me that it was freezing. She said, "Well, we got a horse and buggy and one of those big lap robes and blankets—the children wrapped in big robes—and they drove us back home." She said, "When I heard the news, and they said, most damage was done in the North End of the city—Richmond area." She said, "Well, that's it, I'm going home. I thought my home, my family will be wiped out." All she could think of was, "I've got to get home, I've got to get home."

Mum said somebody ordered her a horse and buggy. A sister told me that she took a taxi. I don't know. It comes to the same thing. Nevertheless, she did get home.

Mum said, "I just prayed, because I could see the devastation as I got nearer the house. I could see it."

She said that when she got home the house was still there, a very solid house surrounded by wrecked or burned houses. People were quickly trying to establish places for soup centres, and they were there at our home trying to get a centre set up in the basement.

When the explosion hit, my father and the children were at home. My father told me—he was in the bathroom, reading his paper.

Helen was ready for school, going out the front door with her friend who lived in the house nearby. The other three were in the kitchen. The girls had been fed, except Viola who was still in the high chair. She had her food in front of her.

"So," he said, "I looked around, everybody seemed fine." The other girls were doing their little drawings and things at their little table, a kids' play table.

Dad told me, "I went in the bathroom, I was reading the paper. I was on the throne when the explosion happened. The bath and the toilet were thrown one way, and the sink went in another direction." And he said, "Oh, my God. Oooohhh." He said, "Oh, the girls!"

My father always went around the house with, as he called them, his braces, his suspenders hanging. Instead of putting them up, he's clutching his pants.

"I came out to the kitchen. I looked. One was on the floor, but she got up, her eyes were open, she seemed fine. Hazel was there, sitting and wide-eyed. Nobody seemed to be hurt. Helen was on the floor, she was lying down."

Dad said, "I looked over at Viola's high chair." He said, "I didn't see any movement. Because one of the window blinds had fallen in on her, and the glass, the pane of glass had fallen in on top of the blind."

On top of Viola.

And Dad said, "I didn't hear a sound. Well, how can I tell Gwen that her child, our child is dead? I'm supposed to be here taking care of them"—that's what Dad told me. "I'm supposed to be here taking care of them." The rationale would be that he couldn't help it. But when that's your child, you figure that you weren't watching.

He said, "I went over there. I prayed—I never prayed—and I lifted the shade up. And she's sitting there," he said, "her eyes were closed." And Dad said, "Viola? Viola?"

And she looked at him and said, "Daddy! Those bad boys, they frowed stones at me!"

And he said, "Thank God."

56

I asked Dad, "What did you do then? What did you do?"

"I bundled them up." He was thinking, "Mum!" His mother lived a block away. "Mum! Mum!"

He had four children and he took them all. He had Viola and Hazel, one under each arm, wrapped up. And he told the others, "You kids, hang on, hang on." Suspenders, the braces. "You take one, and you take the other." And he said, "I was running." He said, "I could see paper, I even saw money." The Bank of Nova Scotia was sort of diagonally opposite them. He said, "I saw those poor people, headless people." My sister told me she saw bodies in the gutter and in the streets.

And Dad said, "I didn't see anything. I saw it after. I gotta go up and see my mother"—and she was only a little four-foot-ten woman. Little Scottish woman. Living with his brother.

Anyway, he walked in the door, and the door was just hanging. And people were running and people were dead. And Dad said, "I didn't realize till I got home that night why I was so tired.

"I opened the door," he said, "I looked in the kitchen. There was glass everywhere. There was the lid of the stove on the floor. My brother was lying on the floor. And my mother was up in the cabinet. Her feet were dangling over the edge." And he said, "Mum, Mum, come down."

"James! James!" she said. "Get William off the floor. What's he doing on the floor? Get him up off the floor."

He said, "I got her down. Told the kids to stay,

'Don't move.' Because the beam was giving way. 'Don't move. Stay right near the corner.' I had one under my arm. I had gotten my mother down. She had a terrible, terrible gash. It should have been stitched."

He said, "Mum. I've got to take you to the hospital. I've got to take you to get help, to get stitches."

"James," she said, "I'm not leaving this house. Get him off the floor. Get him off the floor. Get him sitting up. I'm not having this nonsense in my house. All this foolishness. I'm all right. Get him up off the floor!"

Dad did what he could for her wound. There was glass in it. "And I did wipe it out and cleaned it." She would not leave. He saw a Red Cross flag flying. He gave them the street and house number, that she needed attention. He said, "I've got to get back. I've got to get back." He said, "I'm running through the street."

And when Mum got home, she said she got down on her knees and thanked God. She said, "I feel so guilty. All of the other people have lost so many children." She said, "I felt so guilty feeling so happy that my family was intact."

And that's the day that she was on her way to New Haven.

CHAPTER EIGHT

I Remember My Dad

OUR FAMILY WAS HIT HARD during the Great Depression, perhaps especially my Dad. He started out with his brothers, cutting hair in their father's business, Davis Barber Shop. He worked as a shipwright and even had a car dealership. Eventually he was a landholder, managing property he inherited from his father and property my mother had inherited from hers, collecting rents. But the Depression took the bottom out of everything, and most of the properties were lost, and Dad ended up a proud black man working off and on, such as a car washer at Citadel Motors, and cutting hair at home. Not bad at all, but not where he had been.

Dad felt he could not protect his family as he wanted. He was always aware of his change in status. And he was ever watchful for slights from any quarter and especially anything that he assumed threatened his children.

We lived in a corner house with lots of windows. He had his chair placed so when we went out, he could see where we were going, which way we were coming from. "Okay, be home by such-and-such." He'd time it.

My sister and I—she was next to me in age—she was a little devilish, fun. Anyway, we were coming home from the Casino Theatre, during the war. And behind us were two British sailors. We were both teen-agers—these fellows were behind us, and they were saying something and we were giggling and laughing. Perhaps they thought we were prostitutes.

One of them said to the other one, "Oh!"—with a British accent—"Look at the good-looking black girls!"

What they didn't realize was that we only had this short way to walk and we were home. My father was up in the window. We were laughing and giggling as girls do, being noticed. When we got in our door-way—they were right behind us—my father was there when we opened the door. He grabbed his bat—always had a bat sitting there in the corner of the porch. He told us like this—pointing us inside: "Go."

My father said to the boys, "Can I help you?"

They said, "Oh, I say, do you have any rooms?"

Dad said, "I'll give you rooms!"

He beat them from Gerrish Street almost up to Stadacona—he was running and hitting and beat-ing—and he was a little man! Two sailors! They could have turned on him and killed him! But just his tone, his look! "Go! Go!" He was chasing them.

When he came back, his hair was standing up on

end. My mother said, "Jim! You're going to kill your-self. You're going to have a heart attack."

"They're coming here, insulting my family and me!"

She said, "Let it be. Let it be."

My mother was very gentle. But no sir, Dad sim-mered and stewed. He was like a demon watching out for us.

I WAS A TEENAGER in the 1940s. I was through school, and I was working at the Fisheries Research as a lab technician. I met a boy, through going to dances at Dalhousie University. I started to go out with him. And my father wasn't happy, wasn't happy at all. The boy was from the West Indies, from a completely dif-ferent background, and Dad was very uncomfortable with it.

I asked my mother, "Why is it that Dad doesn't like West Indian students?" My mother tried to ex-plain it very gently to me. It was a long, convoluted explanation that came out over time. It showed how much she loved Dad, no matter what. He would go on tirades and she would just stand there and say, "Jim." Just one word: "Jim." And he'd stop.

Mum said to me, "You have to consider one thing. Your father was just twenty when we got married. He had to get out to work early. He had to leave school in Grade 9. And he could have been other things. You have to realize that he had to work."

She was trying to explain. She knew that every-body has to work. "He wanted to be educated, and he was bright enough to have gone far if he'd had the opportunity. It's different for a woman. He's supposed to be the breadwinner, the family earner. And he feels jealous, and he takes it out in hatred and anger. That's a flaw on his part.

"Your father wanted to be somebody. He wanted to do something. He had the ability. But he was born at the wrong time. And we married too young. He loves his kids. But he doesn't want them going with West Indians because they can offer—they're so full of themselves, that they can do this and that—and that attitude irks your father.

"But their attitude," she said, "is a good attitude to have. I want you to have it, Wanda—not an obnoxious attitude, but an attitude that you can do something, learn any skill. Because they can take anything from you, anything, but they can't take your education. So that's what we want for you."

She knew that my father could be out of line. And he was. One night he tore into one of the students that came to visit me. The fellow went out crying. From St. Lucia. He was a nice, nice person. But Dad saw him as a threat to me as his daughter, to him as a father, to him as a person. And this is only my interpretation.

As she got older, Mum wanted to tell certain things. And, she told me. She told me because I was there. Not because I was so compassionate or understanding. She told just me because she loved me and now there was time to talk, and I was there. That's all.

Dad had Grandfather Davis's example. Grandfather Davis went from his store and barber shop to take the civil service exam—and he became a postman. I'm told he was the first black postman in Halifax.

He had a mail route. He walked. And he walked. And my Dad said to me once, "Guess what my father did on his day off."

I said, "What?"

"Went for long walks!"

So, my grandfather had something. He was a postman and he acquired property. Mum said that in the fall, Grandfather Davis got a load of coal for each married son in the family, and two barrels of apples. When we went down in our basement, you could smell apples. She said he always did that as a gift.

Dad would have liked to be able to do that. And there was a time before the Great Depression when he could. My older sisters remembered him coming to the dinner table dressed in a suit. Then he would take off his jacket, roll up his sleeves and cut the meat. In later years, after the Depression, we were lucky to have meat, and Mum would make it into something like a stew so it would go around.

DAD WAS A HIGHLY INTELLIGENT MAN. Self-taught. He read so much and he absorbed so much. When I was in high school, I always assumed he knew everything. We all did. He read good books. But he also read detective books. Which I read too. Because I loved Ellery Queen—Raymond Burr on TV—and Sam Spade movies. And Agatha Christie. I have the whole set of them upstairs. Hercule Poirot, and Miss Marple. I loved it! I don't read fiction at all, except for that.

Dad and I used to read detective books. And then he'd say to me, "Did you finish it?" Because I'd have one book and he'd have a copy; we'd borrow them from the library. And I said, "Not yet. Don't tell me." He said, "No, I'm not going to tell you. I want you to tell me who you think it is."

We'd do that. We had a rapport that way. And we had other rapports, but that was one of them that I enjoyed.

We used to do the crossword puzzles together.

And he read almanacs, encyclopedias—he would just flip it open and read. And toward his last days—toward the last few years of life—he read the Bible. Every day. I can see him now, sitting with the Bible in his hand. And we buried him with his Bible.

I'LL TELL YOU THIS: My oldest sister, Helen, when she was playing around the house, playing around the yard, she had all these little white girl friends from St. Patrick's School. And Helen always had her own way. And Helen wasn't nasty with it, she was just humorous with it. But she got her own way because she knew how to do it. When it came time to register for school, Helen said, "I'm not going to Alexandra School. I'm going to St. Patrick's." And my mother told her, "Well, you can't go there, dear, because it's just Catholic children that go there."

"Well," she said, "I'm going. I want to go." Stamped her foot. "I want to go."

My father had no problem with Helen going to

an all-white Catholic school, even though we were Protestant.

This little child wanted to join. So she took her catechism lessons from the Sisters. And she became a Catholic. And I don't mean she just became a Catholic that day. She died a Catholic! Her son is Catholic. Her husband was Baptist—but he turned Catholic. She always had her cross; she had her beads all the time. Helen. My oldest sister. Catholic.

Dad said to Mum, "She'll get more out of her life by being around white people, Catholics, than she will around our own people. She'll get more advantages. If she wants to be a nurse, she'll be a nurse."

He felt that they'd see she got in. And at that time black people didn't get into nursing.

MY MOTHER NEVER RAISED HER VOICE. People have this vision, after their parents or anybody they loved, are gone—that they were saints. She wasn't a saint. But when she was speaking to people, if she was annoyed, you knew it. But she didn't raise her voice. She'd be appalled at how some of us speak today.

Mum was from a different era altogether. And from a different, not only era, but background. A Baptist background, yes. But also this gentility that was taught. She had no mother. Her mother, Susan Irene Smith Johnson, died when she was very young. And her father, Reverend H. H. Johnson, left her and her brother with a Mrs. Lucas in Lucasville, outside of Halifax. When her father took his wife's body home to New Haven, Connecticut—she died during his second term as minister in Cornwallis Street Baptist Church in Halifax—he had these two children, a boy and Mum, four and eight years old. He had become quite good friends with the Lucas family.

Mum told me that it was a farming-type place. You know, not a big farm, but a family farm. And her father told the lady, Mrs. Lucas, "I'm going to leave my children with you, for a while. And you must remember to treat them just like your help. They have to help in the fields. They have to help with the animals. They have to help. They're not here as guests."

He paid. I don't know where he got his money, but he had money. They mentioned something about his earnings in Dr. Pearleen Oliver's *A Brief History of the Colored Baptists of Nova Scotia*.

My grandfather bought property while he was in Halifax. He eventually owned property on Swaine Street, North Street, West Street, and John Street. Mum inherited this property; we lived in some of those houses. I was born on Swaine Street.

Mum said that this Mrs. Lucas was very nice, she was just like a mother to her and her brother. And she said she taught Mum how to embroider, and little things like that. And she took her to church.

Reverend Johnson, my grandfather, came back and took Mum and her brother home to New Haven, Connecticut. He looked at his daughter. And of course, she hadn't had much schooling. She had lived out in the boondocks somewhere. And Mum said, "I had the corn sticking out of my ears, practically"—something like that. "I looked like a hick. Sounded like one."

He wanted Mum to keep house for him. But he said he couldn't put her out in the community. She had no manners, no nothing.

So he sent her to the Boston Ladies Finishing School. And of course, that sounds grand. She studied music, and writing, how to write thank-you's, the art of writing, penmanship. And she learned a little bit of poetry. And she learned how to waltz, so she told me. And she had a bit of geography. And, of course, the fundamentals of manners—always manners. *Manners*. And presiding over—not her serving—but being served. "This is the ladies' way."

And she liked it very much. And that's where, as I told you, she learned to dance.

But what happened—my mother visited Mrs. Lucas again. I don't know where she met Dad. Dad and Mum fell in love. Mum would visit Dad's home occasionally. But they were secretly going back and forth. And my uncle, my father's brother, told me, "Yeah, that's when your father was using a bicycle, going out to Lucasville, on a bicycle." And I said something to Dad about bicycling. And he looked at his brother, like, "Big mouth," something like that. "You shouldn't say those things." But he was courting my mother on a bicycle.

They got married—in the Anglican church in Halifax, 1908. Trinity Church, on Cogswell Street. After that she went back home to New Haven, because she was only on a visit. She went back home to her father. And she was supposed to tell him she was married.

"And," she said, "I found out I was pregnant. And

I was serving him"—her father—"serving him in the morning—pork chops and fried potatoes and fried bacon." She said, "I was getting sick. Nauseous. I have to tell him soon."

She was scared to death.

One day her father received a letter from somebody in Halifax, with a clipping cut out of the newspaper—the marriage news section—from the Trinity Church. They mailed it to him. And he was eating one morning. She sat at the table. She was very sick. She had to go to the bathroom. When she came out of the bathroom, he said to her, "Gwendolyn, don't you think it's about time you left and went with your husband?"

So the cat was out of the bag. And he was annoyed.

Her father realized that they were young. She was seventeen, Dad was twenty, going on twenty-one. He said to himself, his daughter found that this was the man she loved and had married. So he was going to try to make it a little easier for them by offering Dad a job. Dad was working here and there. And he wrote my mother and said, "Gwendolyn," he said, "tell James, if he goes to see So-and-so, he can get a job at the CNR, the Canadian National Railways."

And Dad said to Mum, "Do you think I'm going to wait on men, and clean out their spittoons, and shine their shoes? Not on your life."

Mum told me that. He wasn't going to be a porter on a train. I don't think that she told that to anybody else. But she told me.

I Remember My Dad

WHICH REMINDS ME: My sister Helen married when she was eighteen and when I was about two years old. And her husband was away a lot—he was a porter on the railway. And she would come home, asking Mum, "Can I borrow Wanda? Oh," she said, "I miss her. I miss her. I want her. It's just a couple of days."

Mum said, "Well, all right." She knew Helen would take good care of me. And Mum had a lot of kids.

So, off I go to Helen's house.

And the first day I was gone, Dad came home, "Where's Wanda?" Mum said, "Oh, she's at Helen's." Okay.

The second day—"Wanda back?" "Oh, no no no. She's still at Helen's."

The third day Mum said, "Oh, she's still at Helen's."

Dad just wheeled around, put his hat on, and came over and got me, brought me home!

Mum told me, "Your father said, 'That's enough of that! Three days without Wanda!'" Without all the children, you know what I mean. All the children.

YOU KNOW, THERE ARE LITTLE THINGS Dad did for me that were wonderful. As a father. I know that.

I remember when I was in high school, and I used to come home for lunch. It was in the early '40s, war was on. And I'd come around the corner—I think it was the New York Dress Shop in Halifax—and there was this coat in the window and—oh, I'd look at it, you know, "Oh, isn't that beautiful...." To my mother, "Oh, I just saw it, it was camel hair." Actually, it was imitation. And Mum said, "Do you know how much it was?" "Oh, no no, I don't know."

And guess what my father did! My father had those little stamps that you save, wartime savings stamps. Unknown to me, he cashed them in and went down. Then he told me to go down to the store, and find out how much it is. And he told the girl, when I would come in, to let me try on the coat. And then she told me it was paid for. And I got that coat!

You know, little things like that.

WE USED TO HAVE ICE DELIVERED a couple of times a week. Saturday was the big day, because that's when groceries were bought. The ice man would come twice a week, and Saturday was the day my mother would get the newspaper to watch for all the grocery store specials. She would notice, "Oh, pork shoulders"—she would mark out what she'd want.

And she'd say, "I'm going to go down early because meat gets picked over, and I'd like to get some fish."

She'd have everything planned. Dad was home on Saturday—so this was her thing—Saturday morning. And some Saturdays Jackie didn't have to work. We didn't have a car but the store was just down on Gottingen Street, just half a block away from us. And Jackie—that was his job. He had to help Mum home with the groceries.

So Mum cleaned out the icebox. If there was a bit of milk she would leave it to the side to catch any little cold and then empty the basin underneath—that was one of my jobs. And if I came home from school or from work and saw water on the floor—forgot to empty it—the ice had melted and overflowed the drip pan.

So Mum had the icebox nice and clean. And she's sitting now waiting for the man to deliver ice. You can't have him coming without having the stairs clean and the kitchen clean, dishes done.

So this Saturday. Dad used to work on Saturday, when he was called in, so he wasn't home all the time, but this Saturday he happened to be home. Because Mum said, "Gee, he seems to be getting later and later, when he comes."

Dad was reading. "What was that?"

"Lately he's been coming a little later than usual on Saturday."

"He has, has he?"

Mum said, "Well, he has a lot of customers." Mum used to go slowly.

Dad's fuming now. Paper's put down.

Mum said, "If I don't get down there soon it'll all be picked over."

And Jackie wants to go somewhere, and everybody's running around. And I'm sitting there waiting for an explosion!

Okay. The ice man came in. He pulled up in the wagon to the front of the house. And up the steps—a little wizened man. And he had the tongs, carrying a block of ice on his shoulder. And Dad's standing there. Gave him enough room to get up to the top of the stairs.

And he said, "Good afternoon, Mr. Davis. Just move aside till I get this ice...."

"No you don't," said Dad. "I don't want you here with that ice."

"But Mr. Davis."

Dad said, "You are making me sick." He said, "You come here every Saturday. Look at the size of that ice." He said, "When you start out with the white people they have a lovely piece of ice, big piece of ice. We pay the same price for that ice that the sun has been beating down on all day."

"Oh, Mr. Davis, I've got it covered."

"I don't care that you've got it covered. I don't want you back here again. Don't you...."

Mum said, "Jim."

Ice man said, "But Mr. Davis, what will you do for ice?"

Dad said, "Not your concern. Take that ice back and don't ever come back here again. Go."

And the man hesitated. And when he went down the steps, I thought he was going to fall. Because he was tripping, and the ice was dripping.

Mum said, "Now, Jim, what am I supposed to do?"

He said, "Jackie, take your mother down and get your groceries."

He put his hat and his jacket on, and he went down to Glube's. Furniture, everything store—for people in the neighbourhood—because, what was it?—"Dollar down and your life's blood forever." Credit!

One thing my mother always said, "If we can't

afford it—then we can't afford credit. We're not going to get ourselves in debt." She was telling this to all of us. "Just think of what you need, and what you don't need."

Mum didn't know he was going to Glube's. Off he goes.

She's back with groceries. Next thing you know, Glube's truck pulls up—and two men come up with a refrigerator.

Dad told them, "Just put that there. Never mind the pan. We won't have any more drip pans."

They got it all cleaned out, plugged in.

"Now there, Gwen, put your groceries in that." He said, "I paid some money down. And all we have to do...."

Mum: "All we have to do."

"All we have to do"—is pay some amount each week or whatever.

"I told you—you promised me—we were not to go into debt."

He said, "I wasn't having that man here again. Understand that. That man is not coming here, demeaning us with his little bits of ice. There it is. I'll see that it's paid for."

Mum was not happy.

But, after you get used to something. She worried about payments. But it was kind of nice to have a refrigerator. She used to whip up little dessert things that she could never make with the old icebox. You couldn't trust them with a cube of ice; you never really knew the temperature. There she was—gelatins and all sorts of little things with whipped cream. Kind of nice.

But—she never quite relaxed with it. Never, never, never. Because it was hard for them to pay for that. And Mum took care of the money. And Dad said Mum could take a dollar bill and stretch it. But that's if she had the dollar bill. Part of it was going on that refrigerator. She wasn't happy.

It sounds strict but they had to live that way.

They paid it, perhaps missed a couple of payments. But she wasn't happy for a long time. And she controlled the money and where it went, in the house.

They eventually paid for it. They got a couple letters from Glube's. Dad got the letters. I don't know this, but I had a feeling that Viola stepped in and gave Mum a little money to help on the payments. I'm certain it was Viola who finished paying it off.

But Dad didn't do that again. For anything.

It shows the kind of person he was. He would not take any guff from anybody.

AND I KNOW, A FEW YEARS LATER, the girls—my sisters—for some reason, we were celebrating. Came down from Montreal. We were all sitting around talking. And it came to the question: If you were to marry again, would you marry the same man? It was very interesting, what each one said.

And when it came to my mother, she said, "I'd marry the same man, over again. All over again."

CHAPTER NINE

Working in the Fisheries Lab

IN THE FALL OF 1943, I worked at the Fishery Research Board of Canada Halifax Laboratory. It was on-the-job training. And the next summer, they sent me for a chemistry course at Acadia University. "They" meaning the Fishery Research itself, because I just came out of high school. I just had basic chemistry. They wanted to give me a better foundation. They wanted me to become a lab technician. So I went to Acadia for six weeks. It was my first time away from home. I loved the total experience.

When I went to Acadia, I hadn't been anywhere. I had never left my home! And these kids were running around in shorts. So I got a pair of shorts and I was running around too. I studied the chemistry, and came home. The first thing, I went upstairs and I changed, put on my new shorts, and I came downstairs.

My father: "What's that you've got on?" I said,

"Shorts." He said, "Well, young lady, they certainly are shorts. You just take yourself upstairs and put some decent clothing on."

Well, I have to realize he was born in 1885.

IN ANY CASE, I was back home, and well-trained!

During my time with Fisheries, my name appeared on scientific papers with titles like "The Production of Dimethylamine in Mussel and Several Species of Gadoid Fish During Frozen Storage, Especially in Relation to Presence of Dark Muscle," and "The Oxidative Rancidity in Frozen Stored Cod Fillets." But I started out just doing basic, standard techniques in the lab, learning as I went along. The people I worked with were very patient, very kind. My contribution to those scientific papers was the results of the tests that I carried out. Essentially standard lab procedures, which I learned to do, and I did very well. I think anybody could do it, if you're of that inclination—and if you liked it. And I wanted to learn more. So I learned from people around me, the standard procedures, working up to bigger tests to do for the papers, for the men with Ph.D.'s. They had to have somebody there on a lower level to do the basic testing. As I gathered more experience I worked up to more complex test procedures.

I liked it very much. But they were careful to explain to me that results had to be accurate and honest. No fudging; whatever you got was what you got. If you got something that they thought was not right—you started all over again. The scientists in charge of all these experiments were taskmasters, but their name was going to be on the final paper. And they themselves could not do the whole experiment. They had to rely on people like me to get it done. There were a few people who did everything on their own—they might have people come in to wash up their equipment and things like that—but those people were very few.

The work had to be accepted by the scientists in Ottawa. Ottawa was paying us. It had to be done correctly, honestly. I think honesty in results was the first thing that they instilled.

And I got that. I understood that. I liked it. And they were good to me. The salary was quite good.

My mother always said, "When you're going to leave a job, make sure that you leave on a good note"—no rancour, no matter if you feel that you're leaving because of rancour, because of something that happened. Just make sure you're going to leave on a good, friendly note. You never know when you might need those people again.

Truer words have never been spoken.

Because I left that job in December 1948. Got married, went to the States. Ten years later, really in desperate straits, I wrote them a letter and they accepted me back into the lab. And I don't think they would have, if I'd left on a note of sloppy work or insubordination.

But I was extremely lucky because there weren't many good jobs around. And I had no other training since I left Halifax. In the States, I worked at anything. I worked as a nurse's attendant and nurse's aide, and the five-and-ten sales girl, and I scrubbed floors. I did what I had to do. But I did nothing related to research or my training in Fisheries.

I might as well say it here—that I came back to Halifax when I left my husband, came back with the three children. I wanted to come home. But the only reason I came home was that job waiting for me. I did not want to burden my parents. I wrote Fisheries a month or so before I left the States. Apparently my former boss said, "If it is the Wanda that we know, she's welcome to have a job in my department." So the job was waiting for me when I came back

It was now a microbiology department, and I didn't have to re-train because I knew the basic work in a research lab.

But I don't know what I would have done without my parents. Because to have a job is one thing. But now I had three children, two of them were school-aged. One of them was definitely not. Without my parents, I don't know how I could have done it.

Viola did not want me to do this, because Mum and Dad were aging. I thought about getting an apartment by myself and trying to work things out. And Mum said, "I wouldn't have had it any other way." She said, "That's what families are about. Don't you worry about Viola, she'll come around."

My father didn't seem to mind. I'm being truthful, because this man was short of temper, and things exasperated him. Maybe aging had mellowed him a bit.

Every now and then I'd see him look at my son

Jeff with a smile on his face. Jeff was my youngest. Dad would say to Jeff, "Wait for me, old-timer, I'm coming." And they got along famously. Dad called Jeff "old-timer."

They had jokes back and forth. And Dad used to talk politics to Jeff. About Diefenbaker. And he said, "Well, old-timer, looks like they're after our man again." Jeff would say, "Diefenbake?" "Yeah, Diefenbaker." And Dad said, "You know what? He's coming in on the train, down there at the CN station. Would you like to meet him?" Jeff said, "Yes." But they never did get down. I think Dad wasn't feeling well that day so they didn't get down.

But he would read the news to Jeff. "What are they doing to Diefenbake?" They got along famously.

While I was working, Mum was more the one who raised my children. I could see it when I came home. She'd say, "I've got the children all fed, so you can sit down and have a meal quietly. They're going to go do their homework. I've got that set up."

So I'd have my supper and the children would be finishing their homework. Then they were getting tired, but they're roughhousing and running around upstairs. And I'd be on the phone, like a teenager, talking to one of the girls at work. We even did exercises on the phone! And she was, like, eighteen, and I was thirty-something. And she was a friend of mine.

Anyway, Mum said, "You should get those children to bed earlier." Well, early to her meant no later than eight o'clock. "I will, Mum, I will." I think, when I got home, I relaxed. Instead of keeping on my treadmill of doing what I had to do, get them to bed, and then relax. But her idea was to get home, get supper, get the kids a bath—in bed. Run, run, one, two. I would do it, but by the time I got through it was past 8:30, and Mum, well—she didn't say too much, but she didn't like it. She reprimanded me very gently.

The only time that she ever said anything that drew me up by my bootstraps was when my husband and I came home from the States in 1952 for him to play the summer baseball season. I had the one child then. He was teething. Oh, he was in terrible shape. Nine or ten months old. Stevie. I was up half the night with him, rocking back and forth. Of course my husband wasn't home. That's another story. And I'd be in the room, rocking back and forth.

My mother came in, and I was whining "Mum!" A twenty-six-year-old woman. Whining. She said, "Give him to me." And then she turned around and she said, "Grow up! And stop crying to me!"

Of course! She'd been through that all her life! Teething and full diapers and throwing up, and whining! Fifteen children. And here I've got one child, and I'm whining to her, "He won't sleep and I'm so tired." She said, "Grow up!"

And about nine years later, I came back. No husband. I have three children. And my family accepted us. At least they made me comfortable enough that I could spend the day out earning a living. Truthfully, I don't know why Mum said yes. I really don't know what I would have done without her.

But Mum knew that I would take care of my children, and pay my debts, and not go into debt. She was willing to be there for the children during the day. If anything happened, she knew I'd come home.

I had holidays and weekends off. I had three weeks in the summer. One week I would take them to Montreal, visit my sisters, and my boys could meet their cousins.

I WAS VERY PROUD of my work in the Fisheries Lab.

Mr. Castell made a big contribution to the fresh fish industry. He used to go out in the morning—he'd note the day and the time. He'd go down to the Fishermen's Market on the wharf, and meet the vessels that came in. He'd get samples of what should be fresh fish. They didn't know what he was doing. He was just somebody buying fish for the day. He would go to three or four establishments, and from the boats—anywhere they sold fish.

He was very meticulous. He'd have to be, to be credible. He would buy different kinds of fish. And he'd go down twice a week. And he would go at different times. Get something at the beginning of the day, and at the end of the day.

And then he'd come back to the lab. He'd take a sample of each fish right away, put it in different small beakers. These beakers would come to me. I would know what kind of fish they were, but I didn't know under what conditions they had been stored before they were sold. Whether they were held in ice, or just put out there under glass in the market.

He sometimes had up to three people working for him. One would do protein analysis. The other would do rancidity tests. The stronger the colour the higher the rate of rancidity. They were standard tests. You ran them against a control sample, compared them.

Some samples were tested in the cold lab. I wore gloves like pianist Glenn Gould, with the tips of the fingers off.

But most important, I had a job. I had a government job. And I liked the job. Actually, when I first started, the Atlantic Fisheries Experimental Station was looking for a young man—a high school graduate, whose marks, particularly in science, were good. But when I started, young men at that time were going off to war. They wanted somebody in the teenage bracket—so, they chose a young girl.

WE WERE CONCERNED with the condition of the fish. They ran taste panels. They had a kitchen. The fish samples were all coded. They gave me a form. Somebody in the kitchen cooked the fish, always the same way. And then they'd give each person four to six samples. And they were just numbered 1, 2, 3, or A, B, C.

And you checked off condition of the fish—was it soft? Was it solid? Did it have a lot of bones? The colour of the fish. Then the flakiness, and then the final thing—there's more categories, but the final thing—is your taste. You eat it. And I used to hit it ninety-eight percent of the time. I could tell which one was the freshest. Which one was the next, the next, the next.

I was one of the better tasters. One of the samples was a control sample. Nothing done to it but cooked. And I could pick it out.

We had a goal. Mr. Castell had a goal. As a government employee, he hoped to have better fish sold. Fish sold to the public, under honest, better conditions. He wanted our findings sent to Ottawa so fishermen would be careful on trawlers, on how they stored their fish before it came into port. He would find conditions that were filthy. Or they'd lay fish out there in the sun. Fish deteriorate very quickly.

Before the 1950s, fish caught offshore were stored on the boat, usually with no ice or cooling process. But if you want to sell fish, you want to get the name of having good fish. Fish coming almost from the water jumping into your mouth. That was his goal. To make trawler captains and merchants more aware, and not so careless in the storage of fish, because it's important. It's important to the public. It's only fair. Even more than fair—that's not quite the word. But you know what I mean. He was a responsible public servant.

CHAPTER TEN

Ten Years
in the
United States

I'M NOT GOING TO DISCUSS my first marriage in any detail, except to offer the excuse of naivety. Still, I have to say something, otherwise why did I go back to Halifax after ten years in the U.S.A., with three lovely sons in tow? Three sons and a cat! But the fact is, I still have some anger—anger at him and a little anger at myself.

I was twenty-one and star-struck. He was a baseball player for the professional farm team of the Brooklyn Dodgers. When he came to Nova Scotia to play the summer, the girls went wild. Whatever it was I saw in him, I called it love. But you couldn't fool my Dad. While Dad was quick to judge, I think he had this guy pegged from the beginning.

Here's just one telling incident: When I met the

baseball player, my mother was ill in the hospital. That is how, probably, that this relationship was allowed to get out of hand. I didn't have my mother. And it's not that I was a baby. But my Mum had monitored my coming and going without my realizing.

So it happened that she had not yet met him. My father was busy running back and forth to the hospital. So I was free! When Mum came home from the hospital, I said to my new boyfriend, "My mum's home now." He went to the florist and purchased a bouquet of flowers and came to the house.

She was in her bedroom. Dad was standing there. I introduced them. He handed Mum the flowers. She said, "Oh, those are very nice. Thank you. Wanda, would you get a vase."

He looked at her and said, "Those aren't the ones I ordered! The ones I ordered were much bigger, fuller."

"Oh," my mum said, "they're lovely."

He said, "I'm going to go back and—"

"Don't change them," she said. "They're fine."

And after he left, my father burst out laughing. He said, "Did you hear that nonsense?"

I asked, "What nonsense?"

"He's a liar! A liar. He wanted to impress your mother, so he lied about flowers."

In my mind all I could think was, Why would anybody lie about flowers?

And Dad said, "Oh, God help you, Wanda." He said, "He's lying, wanted to make himself look better. He's cheap. He's a liar. And when you find someone who will lie about that, they'll lie about anything."

And I was so naïve.

THERE WERE OTHER SIGNS that should have told me to take the nearest exit fast.

Once we got to the States, I made great friends. I was living with his grandparents, and I was working in a private nursing home. I had two jobs. I also worked in Woolworth's 5-and-10 when they would call me. I had to work. I didn't have any money. He'd gone off, in training somewhere. And he never sent money home.

One time, he called me, and he said, "I'm really short of money." I said, "Well, so am I." "Could you send me a couple of dollars," he said, "I'll send it back."

So I sent him all I could—a ten-dollar money order. You'll never guess what happened. The post office police came to my workplace. "Did you send a postal order to this person?" I said, "Yes." He said, "How much?" "Ten dollars." He said, "Ten dollars?" I said, "Yes."

My husband had put an extra zero on that money order. He cashed it for a hundred dollars. They knew I didn't do that. But they couldn't prove that he did it either.

And it continued. One night he came running in, pounding on the door. He was wet, his feet were wet. And he went in the bathroom and took off his shoes and socks, put on his slippers, and grabbed up our son.

"If anybody comes in that door, I've been here all night."

Pounding on the door! Police. My parents—we

never had police coming to our door. He told them he'd been in all night. I had my back turned; I didn't say anything. I said to myself, "I'm not saying for or against." They didn't ask and I didn't say a word.

But that's just icing on the cake.

FOR A WHILE, we were living in a rented house. I had given my husband the rent money. The man came to me for the rent. My husband had spent my money. It was like a nightmare.

And wife-swapping! This woman—the wife of one of the other players—invited me out to lunch. I had no idea what she was talking about. She had a child, and I had a child. The men were playing baseball out of town. She kept talking, and I thought—I don't know what she is talking about. I finally got it when she said, "You know, I always wanted to go with a black man."

Don't tell me! I got the message, and I got out of there quickly.

I realized that he was playing around. And I complained to his mother. She just said, "I'll tell you what you do. You go out and you find yourself a boy friend."

Oh, I was altogether too far from my home in Halifax! I had my cocoon on Gottingen Street. I probably thought it was a prison then, when you're younger, but you know where to go. I had a home there, and all I had to do was open the door and I knew what Mum was cooking! Smelled good! Cornbread.

AFTER MY SECOND SON WAS BORN, I wasn't able

to work, and we moved to another house. I took care of two other children at home, to make some money, to pay for our rent.

When I was pregnant again, I could only take odd jobs, like at the church, when they had meetings and big food functions. I went in after, take my little cart down, wash all the dishes. And I worked at the 5-and-10 part time. Anywhere I could get a few dollars. That's how we subsisted.

We had no money. My husband's uncle used to come now and then and fill the fridge with food. The day I brought the third child home from the hospital, my husband had to run around selling bottles to get money for milk, for baby Jeff. That's the way it was.

I went to the town hall, to social services. I said, "I have three children now. I worked all the time I could. But I can't anymore. So I can't feed them, and I have rent to pay."

That's when the lady in charge of the social services said, "Why should we take care of *his* children? He drives a Cadillac." Everyone knew him in that small town.

I said, "Well, I don't have anything."

She said, "Well, women like you annoy me. Because you let your husband do anything, and you expect the town to pay for his children."

"I'm at the end of my rope, and I need medical attention." I started to go out the door.

She said, "I can't see you go out like that." And she gave me a slip for groceries.

And later I had to go back. By this time, my hus-

Wanda Davis Robson at age 16; and Wanda out for an evening with her
sister, Viola Irene Davis Desmond (on the right)

James Albert Davis and his wife, Gwendolyn Irene Johnson Davis

Wanda Robson at work at the Fisheries Research Halifax Laboratory. Below left, an example of the research papers to which Wanda's work made a contribution. Below right: Viola Desmond during the Second World war. Note the "V for Victory" brooch.

ENVIRONMENT CANADA

FISHERIES AND MARINE SERVICE

HALIFAX LABORATORY   HALIFAX, NOVA SCOTIA

E.G. BLIGH, DIRECTOR

NEW SERIES CIRCULAR NO. **44**   MARCH 22, 1974

THE MEASUREMENT OF THE BONE CONTENT IN MINCED FISH FLESH
-J.R. DINGLE, W.D. AUBUT, D.W. LEMON AND WANDA ROBSON-

Introduction
    Meat separators are being increasingly used to recover edible flesh from previously unused species of fish and from the residue of filleting operations. In one type of machine, the raw material is squeezed between a belt and a perforated metal drum moving at different speeds, and this results in the softer parts such as the flesh being extruded through the holes of the drum, whilst the harder or tougher parts, like bone and skin, are passed on to discard. In another type, called a strainer, the material is forced by a worm-feed into a perforated drum, so that the flesh is forced through the holes and unwanted material is discharged through an opening at the end of the drum. The separation of flesh is not perfect in either machine, and some small pieces of bone and skin will be found in the product, in size and amount depending on the size of the holes in the drum, as well as other operating conditions, and on the nature of the raw material. Bones left in the product, and particularly the presence of large bones or bone particles is a major quality defect influencing the consumer acceptability of cooked products made from the minced flesh. Several reported methods for estimating bone content in comminuted flesh of chicken, crabs, etc. have been examined, and a modification of an AOAC procedure for determining shell in crab meat seems to provide a readily applicable method for use with minced fish flesh. It should be particularly effective for quality control,

band's moved—gone. So, to the social services: "I don't have any heat. I don't have any lights, because he didn't pay." And this time she said, "That's not our problem."

SO VIOLA CAME TO MASSACHUSETTS, came from New York. She was studying beauty culture there, and working part time. She knew I was in trouble because my mother phoned her or wrote to her, and said that she hadn't heard from me for quite a while. It wasn't like me not to write.

Viola took one look and said that this will never do. "You can't live this way." No lights and no heat. And I was heating with a little black pot-bellied stove, set up in front of my electric stove. Somebody helped me put the pipes up. And that's how I cooked dinner, got heat, and everything.

Viola said, "It's going to be cold soon. It's fall." She said, "You're all going to die, because this is a death trap. It's not put up right. Those pipes weren't meant for this. The kids are going to get burned up."

She said, "I'm going to the town hall." I said, "It's Saturday. They won't be open."

She went to the town hall. Inside, she found a meeting going on. She opened the door and said, "I want to speak to the head of social services."

The mayor told her, "You can't come in. We're having a meeting."

And Viola said, "Oh, yes I can. Yes I can. I can come in here, because I have something to say. It's about my sister." And she named me.

This woman stood up, and Viola said, "So you're

that woman." And she said, "First of all, you were very rude to my sister." She said, "You pick on women who cannot defend themselves. The vulnerable women. How dare you!"

Viola turned to the mayor and said, "My sister's living down there. No heat, no lights. It doesn't matter whose fault it is. She has children."

And the Mayor said, "Well—we can't discuss that right now—because it's the weekend, and we'll have to deal with that the first of the week."

And Viola said to him, "Well, children die on the weekend too."

The meeting was adjourned.

When she got back to where I lived, there was a truck there already. Lights were on. And they were fixing the stove.

VIOLA HELPED DIFFERENT FAMILY MEMBERS. She told them, "It's not charity. You can pay me back when you get it." And when her will was read, she left every nephew and niece money to start their education. Every one. Every one.

She didn't have any children—she wanted to have a child. But I don't know how she would have fitted a child into her busy life. I don't know how she would have done that. So, she wanted to adopt one of my children. She had a plan whereby she would ask my sisters to adopt the other two boys. I don't think she ever actually discussed this with them. She said, "I offer that as a solution. And I will pay your complete expenses for you to go to college, whatever you want to take. To Dalhousie, or wherever you want to go, I'll pay for it."

Anyhow, I thought about it briefly. I didn't want to give up my kids. I just couldn't. Viola thought I was being very selfish.

In any case, the woman who took care of social assistance, she gave me the lowest amount of money she could give on the scale. I couldn't get any money out of my husband. And she said, "Oh, yes you can. You just sign for a warrant for his arrest for non-support."

I didn't want to do that but eventually I did. I had to.

I remember him standing there in court with four or five other men. The judge came in. He was a little Italian man. He was small. And he was sick. He had cancer. But he came in. And he glared. He said, "You know something?" he said. "I don't want to be here today, but I am. And you know what? I'm sick and tired of hearing you men whining, while your wives and children are starving, and while you expect everybody else to pay for them. You, you, you, you, let me hear your story. Actually," he said, "I don't want to hear your story." He said, "Here it is right here in black and white. What can you say?" And he continued, "All of you should be ashamed of yourselves. I don't feel very well today." And he said, "I don't want to hear all your lies.

"The bottom line is that you've got children. Who do you think is supposed to take care of those children? What did you bring them into the world for? They're yours to support, and you are going to pay for it. Now." And he gave them all six months in jail.

My husband went to jail! And that meant trouble for me.

He was angry, angry!

But, I couldn't go on. Viola said, "You can't go on this way."

So they increased my money.

Viola said, "Okay. You decide what you're going to do." She said, "You work on getting a separation while he's in jail." She said, "I'll be back before he's out. Because you're not staying here."

The Red Feather Agency gave assistance to single parents. And they gave me a lawyer. He charged twenty-five dollars when it was all over. Best twenty-five dollars I ever spent.

He said to me, "You are going to receive a letter very soon. From your husband. I know their style. They get together in jail, they talk. How they can beat this system, and beat the little woman down.

"First thing you're going to get, very soon, is a letter. A love letter. He loves you. He wants you. He loves the kids." He said, "Don't get me wrong. I'm not here to break up marriages—but you haven't got a marriage."

He said, "We work now. You want a formal separation now. That way, when he steps out of jail, he has no place to go except to his mother or wherever. He wants to come back with you. You and the kids are a haven.

"Now," he said, "when you get the letter, I'm telling

you not to answer it. But you do what you want."

So I got the letter. He loved me! I didn't answer it.

So the next one was a love letter, but not quite as passionate. By third or fourth letter: "I'm gonna get you when I get out. You're gonna be sorry—!"

If the wife agrees that her husband has a place to go, he can be released earlier and live back at home, and they let them out. And he was working toward that.

When he got out at the end of his six months, he was furious. The lawyer and I had talked it over. He asked me, "Do you have a place to go? Can you leave without a backward glance, take your three children and go?" I said, "Yes. My father and mother said, 'Come home.'"

I had already written to the Fisheries Lab in Halifax; they had a job waiting for me. There was a God!

My three children were American citizens, and I'm Canadian. I might be stopped at the border. There was one more hearing before the divorce, about the children. The lawyer asked me, "Can you walk away? Now?"

He said he would go to court for me.

I just picked up and left. I got on the Boston train, came to Halifax. The lawyer wrote me a letter saying that the judge said, "I want you to tell her that I don't know why she didn't do it sooner."

The divorce was granted.

CHAPTER ELEVEN

Viola Desmond and the Roseland Theatre

THE STORY OF THE INCIDENT at the Roseland Theatre in New Glasgow, November 8, 1946, starts out like any good storytelling. A beautiful young woman, thirty-two years old, is driving alone from Halifax to Sydney. She is carrying a line of her own beauty products that she plans to deliver, her head full of dreams for her growing business—and the car breaks down. The repairman in New Glasgow tells her they won't have the part until the next day. Suddenly for this businesswoman, Viola Desmond, the pressure is off. She can't go on to Sydney until tomorrow. She realizes that she has free time before dinner, before she finds a place for the night.

Viola said—this is Viola telling me—she said to herself, "I'll call Dad and Mum that I will be here overnight. Because I won't be in Sydney, they might worry."

But she said before she saw anyplace for a phone, "Oh, there's a movie." The movie at the Roseland Theatre was *The Dark Mirror* starring Olivia de Havilland. She really liked Olivia de Havilland. And Lew Ayres was in it—a fine actor. "Aah. A chance to sit down and go to a movie." Whether the movie was murder or love or whatever, it was a movie, to sit in the dark and be warm. And relax!

Because Viola had disciplined herself not to relax. Not to really relax. I find that kind of sad, but that's the way she was. She would do what she wanted to do, get it done. She would not have given herself a break, if her car hadn't broken down.

I think, for just a moment, Viola was off-guard. Viola did not have many moments where she could just relax, and not think of the next customer, not think of anything at all except herself, and enjoy. I think she was a strict taskmaster, hard on herself. I think she didn't allow herself time to enjoy. This is not to show a good side of her, and not a bad side of her—but gee, where's the fun? Where do you get a little life? But it was her choice.

I know she loved to go to movies. When she had a chance, she and her husband Jack liked to go and see a movie.

I'm sure she wasn't dressed for the weather. Mum said Viola never dressed warmly enough. She lived within a block of her beauty parlour. She'd put on her fur coat and her fur overshoes. She didn't have bare legs, she wore nylons. Women didn't wear slacks then. Maybe around the house, but they didn't wear slacks outside. Not if they were ladies. Viola certainly never wore them anyway. In any case, she would just run up to the beauty parlour.

Anyway, she said, "When I walked in, it felt cozy." And I think, when you walk into a theatre and you feel the warmth, you begin to relax. And it was a cold, frosty night. There was a girl in a little glass cage. Viola said, "I'll have one ticket, please."

So the girl looked at her and gave her a ticket, and gave her the change. She went in, and she said, "I sat down in the lower level. Oh, it was so nice to sit down. I stretched my legs out. And the movie was just about beginning. I looked up and I saw"—the actors, the opening credits.

"Then I felt this tap on my shoulder. And," she said, "the usher, the girl, said, 'Miss, you can't sit here.'"

Viola said, "Well, why not?"

She said, "Well, your ticket is for balcony, upstairs, so you'll have to go upstairs."

So Viola figured, "Well, I'll just give her the difference between downstairs and upstairs, then I'll go back to my seat."

So she went to the ticket booth and she said, "I'd like to change this ticket for a downstairs ticket." And so, she said, the girl stopped, and looked at her. And the girl said, "Well, we're not allowed to sell tickets—downstairs tickets—to you people."

Viola said—it just hit her—"You people."

Viola Desmond and the Roseland Theatre

So Viola told her, "Well, there is the money. And I am going to sit downstairs. Because I'm very short. And my sight is not good. And I always sit downstairs in a movie."

Had this been a movie theatre in Halifax, there wouldn't have been an issue. She herself mentioned that. I don't remember having any trouble going to the movies in Halifax—sit where you want.

And I'm confident, as Dr. Constance Backhouse wrote about it in *Color-Coded: A Legal History of Racism in Canada, 1900-1950*, that what happened next was spontaneous.

I really don't think it was something that Viola thought out, certainly not before she was in the thick of it. I don't think so. Because I think it hit her, all of a sudden, when she heard "not allowed" and "you people."

Because she always sat downstairs in the Halifax theatres, so that's where she went this night.

She went back into the theatre, back to her downstairs seat. Viola told me, "I started to relax. I was getting a little frustrated. I wanted to watch the movie." So, in a minute again, the usher is back. "Miss, you really can't sit here." She said, "If you don't move, I'll have to call the manager."

Viola said, "I'm not doing anything wrong. You can call the manager." And she settled down again. "And," she said, "the manager came. Mr. MacNeil. And he said, 'You've been told that you can't sit here.'"

So Viola said, "I'm not causing any trouble." She said, "I offered the girl the difference in the pay, and she refused my money. I left the money on her counter. I have to sit downstairs."

Anyway, the manager said, "Well, if you don't move, I'm going to have to get a policeman."

"Well," Viola said, "get a policeman. I'm doing nothing wrong." As she said later on, "I didn't see any sign that said, 'Coloured people are not allowed downstairs. You go upstairs.' I never saw any sign. So," she said, "I sat down. And a few—about five minutes later—I was really getting into the movie now."

She said, "Here they come, the two of them—one policeman, and Mr. MacNeil. And he said, 'For the last time, are you going to move?' I said, 'No. I am not moving.'"

So one took one arm, and one took the other arm, and—it wouldn't be very difficult to drag her out. She was ninety-five or ninety-six pounds. So they dragged her out to the door. And she said, "I just sort of went limp, because I wasn't going to make it easy for them." And then, she said, one shoe dragged off, and she dropped her purse. And one woman that was sitting down in the lower part of the theatre ran up behind her and gave her her purse, and put her shoe up on top of the purse. Viola looked at her face, and she looked disturbed. And the woman said, "Oh dear, oh dear," or something like that. And sat down.

Viola went out. They dragged her out to the door.

"Actually," she said, "when I came to the doorway, I just put my hand out like that," holding onto the door—to the sides. "And," she said, "they pried my fingers loose. Because I wasn't going willingly. I was not going willingly."

I THINK VIOLA HELD HER GROUND because she was Viola. She was standing up for Viola more than anything. She was a prim, light-skinned woman, and really she did not get around very much, and I think issues of segregation were far from her mind. I don't think she witnessed much—she certainly had been told stories, about instances of racism—but I don't think in Halifax she experienced anything, personally. In the United States she did—but in Halifax she didn't get out around. She did very little shopping. Once she was married, her husband bought all the groceries. And when she went shopping for clothing, Mum was with her—and while Mum considered herself coloured, Mum certainly looked white.

When she shopped for clothes, Viola always took Mum because Mum had a sharp eye for clothing that would work for Viola. Viola was very short, four foot eleven. And Mum could adapt clothes. She was a great seamstress. And Viola was very demanding, wanted her hemline level. She always insisted that she had one hip higher than the other.

Perhaps because of that hip she would not even consider climbing stairs to the balcony of the movie theatre. Besides, she always said she liked to sit downstairs, she liked to get close to the movie screen. Because of her vision.

Viola certainly knew about racial issues. She served other black women every day. And in among the beauty parlour talk—they'd be laughing and talking about what was going on, who's going to the dance, and who's getting married and who's having a baby—Viola would hear what life was like for an ordinary black woman in Halifax.

Now, a skilled black doctor could not see his patients in the Victoria General Hospital and black girls could not go into nursing and black women could not have their hair washed or curled or coifed in most beauty parlours in Halifax. Nothing written—these were not laws. But you could sit where you wanted in a Halifax movie theatre.

ANYWAY, VIOLA SAID, when they got outside the Roseland, Mr. MacNeil got in a car and left. He left to get an order for her arrest from a judge. The policeman got a taxi and took her to jail. When they reached the jail, Mr. MacNeil came running in with the order that she had to be held in jail. Viola said, "I saw the matron's face. She was really disturbed." But still, Viola was put into a cell.

I asked her what her cell was like. "Everything was sort of gray. My own feeling—I felt gray!" There was some kind of a cot in the corner, against the wall. And it had a pillow. And a blanket. And I think she said there was a little sink where you could wash your hands or whatever.

I said, "Did you lie down?"

"Oh, dear, no," she said, "I wouldn't lie down there."

She stayed up all night. She may have closed her

eyes, but I know she sat there. She said, "I braced my back against the wall. Got my purse out, and I decided that I'd clean up my purse, get my appointment book ready. See who was due to come in the first of the week."

She said, "I got out my appointment book." She meticulously went over what she had done and what she should do. This was Friday. "I won't be there Saturday. Did I tell Rose about the children coming in?" Rose Gannon Dixon was the girl that she had trained, the one she depended on. Rose had gone to Viola's school—the Desmond School of Beauty Culture—and graduated. And she stayed on and worked with Viola—a hardworking, very nice girl.

Years later, remembering, Rose said that she learned a lot from Viola. Viola was such a fair person with her. She had a wage every week. And Rose said, those times, young black girls didn't have steady jobs like that.

And in the cell, Viola planned the week ahead, and then she dumped out her purse, organizing it.

Through it all, she said, "I put my gloves on." Viola was a lady, she loved her gloves. And she said to me one time, "You know, it's nice being ladylike and wearing white gloves. But I'll let you in on a little secret. My hands are so bad, that I thank the Lord and my mother for wearing gloves!"

People thought the white gloves were just to look chic. Perhaps she would have worn them anyway. But she wore those gloves because her hands had become work hands, her skin was rough and hard. "That's from my work. The chemicals." Otherwise, she had soft, nice skin. But her hands looked older.

She was alone in the cell but there were other cells. And it was Friday night, and she could hear the men being put in cells. And when they realized there was a woman there—this is one of the things she said that I want to block out of my mind—their suggestive remarks. The matron told them to stop, cut it out, and be quiet. And some of them were drunk.

"You could hear them coming in through the night, mumbling," Viola said. "The matron was very nice and she seemed to realize that I shouldn't have been there. I was jailed for twelve hours."

So, it wasn't a great atmosphere. "But what do you expect?" she said. "It's a jail. And," she said, "I kept saying to myself, 'What am I doing here?'" Like she was telling Dad this, later: "I said, 'What have I done wrong?'"

VIOLA SPENT THE WHOLE NIGHT in the cell. The next day—she was taken from the cell to the courtroom. This is the point where I think she should have had someone with her, someone to speak for her. But—not even a phone call.

The theatre manager and the police officer were there, also the usher and the ticket seller. And there was the magistrate. Viola had no lawyer. The witnesses said that Viola had purchased an upstairs balcony ticket and then took a seat downstairs. They said that by doing that, by paying only the cheaper balcony ticket, she had defrauded the provincial government of the difference in the amount of amusement tax charged. The tax was three cents downstairs, and two cents upstairs. The unpaid difference was one cent. That was the case.

The judge asked, "Mrs. Desmond, is this true?" Well, she gave them her account of what happened. And the judge said, "Well, you didn't pay the amusement tax."

The magistrate asked her if she had any questions. She said later, "I did not gather until almost the end of the case that he meant questions to be asked of the witnesses. It was never explained to me of whom I was to ask the questions." So the witnesses were not cross-examined.

And more important, the racial issues underlying the entire event were never brought up in court. The whole trial was based on the manager's claim that she refused to pay the one cent of amusement tax. And no part of the court documents mentions the race-based seating arrangements in that theatre.

The magistrate said, "You didn't pay the difference in the price." Viola said, "Well, I tried to. I offered. It was refused."

So, she was declared guilty of not paying the full amusement tax due on a first floor seat. One cent.

And as I understand it, she tried to explain, but when she said "but"—she was cut off. She didn't realize she should have had someone with her, some legal advice. That she could have had someone with her to either stay the case for a time, have it gone over again, or else in some other way work for her, or talk for her. She seemed so confident that being right would carry the day. I don't understand it—because she was an intelligent woman. Because ordinarily she could manage things, deal with people. Her business was a success and already, to younger women, she was an inspiration.

But that day, she was sleep-deprived and upset. So. Guilty. And fined the lowest amount allowed by law—twenty dollars. Plus six dollars costs that went to the theatre manager, that Mr. MacNeil.

Viola told Dad the next day, "I tried to tell them...." And Dad said something like, "You should have had someone with you or for you. Where have you been? You can't go to court and say, 'I didn't do it,' and expect them to say, 'Well, that's okay, you didn't do it,' and let you go. You have to have proof of innocence."

WHEN VIOLA LEFT THE COURT, she did not continue on to Sydney. Dr. Backhouse asked me years ago, "Why do you think she didn't get in her car and complete her journey?"

Well, I think that Viola was bitterly disappointed. She even said she was disappointed when she got home. And I don't think she was feeling that well physically after the way that things went. And for the first time, I don't think her heart was in business, in going on.

You know what I think? You know, it's funny; I never thought of this until recently. I think she reverted to being a child again. I think she just wanted to go home to Mum and Dad. If I told her that, she'd say, "Oh, no, I don't think so." But, I really think, when things get down, no matter how old you are, I really think maybe Mum and Dad is the best place—even for a few hours—to get you back on your feet.

And I don't think Viola ever before felt like she needed to get back on her feet. But this was a blow to her. A blow to her physically. A blow to her as a businesswoman. And as a woman of pride.

This was some unfinished business, through no fault of her own.

VIOLA HAD MADE UP HER MIND what she wanted to do with her life, and she was going to do it. You know, come hell or high water, she was going to do it.

I could feel Viola's strength. I really could, at times. I know, because I don't have it—never did, and never will—have her strength. And suddenly, she didn't have strength—this strength that I'm talking about—to get her stuff ready, all her commodities and her things for sale—and carry on to Sydney.

That was a matter-of-fact thing. And when that was interrupted—and so unexpectedly. She got in the car, she just had to go home. She turned back. She came home.

She talked with Dad. And she saw our family doctor about the bruises. He was a very good doctor and a wonderful man. Dr. Alfred E. Waddell. And actually, his gravesite is right by my parents'. He was from Trinidad, and because of his colour he was not allowed to practice at the hospital. He strongly advised Viola to see a lawyer about her injuries. And Viola thought about this.

Viola was distressed. She went to see Pearleen Oliver and it was really Mrs. Oliver who got Viola rolling. Pearleen had fought other battles for racial equality and justice, and especially for preserving black history and culture. Pearleen urged Viola to allow the Nova Scotia Association for the Advancement of Coloured People to take up her case.

Pearleen Oliver encouraged Viola to get a lawyer. The NSAACP was young. It was organized only about a year earlier. And it took some convincing, because there were people in the NSAACP who did not think where you sat in a movie theatre should be their issue, that it wasn't important enough. But Pearleen convinced them, and a Viola Desmond Court Fund was created. Viola's case, presented before the Supreme Court of Nova Scotia, was an important step that the NSAACP took to assist coloured people.

Carrie Best's newspaper, *The Clarion*—a Nova Scotian newspaper for coloured people—got behind her. Mrs. Best was one of Viola's customers. *The Clarion* of December 31, 1946, featured a photo of Viola on the first page and an article about the incident, and also another article about a planned meeting in Halifax to help fundraise.

I go back to Dr. Backhouse's book. Because sometimes I'm not sure of things. And over time you do forget things. I don't want to be wrong. Dr. Backhouse's book *Color-Coded* is very thorough. She shows why the Supreme Court case was dismissed on a technicality.

I think she indicated that Viola's lawyer, Bissett, felt the failure. Perhaps he knew that he handled it badly, too cautiously. Again, the racial issue never came to the fore. And I understand his fee was donated to the NSAACP.

Throughout the trial, race was never mentioned. And it took the *Halifax Chronicle* to point out that Viola Desmond "was tried for being a negress."

I SHOULD KNOW MORE. I certainly had the opportunity to talk with Viola—but I didn't. I did ask her, "How was the cell?" But really, when I heard "Your sister went to jail!"—well, my reaction was not mature. Otherwise, I would have sat down with her, find the time when she came in for a snack from work, get more details.

But I didn't, because the word "jail" made me think, for that moment, that Viola was a lesser person than our family was brought up to be. And of course, that was not right. I knew she had done nothing wrong. But all I could think about was her being in jail. And today I regret that—not talking to her more about the incident. Because I could have gotten more of Viola's ideas about it all. Her feelings.

I know she was disappointed. I think she reserved her inner thoughts, or anything personal, for Carrie Best and Pearleen Oliver. And the singer Portia White; she came to the beauty parlour at special hours, because of her tour schedules. Viola had just two or three people she would confide in.

She might have told me more, had I asked. But I

did not ask. I did not want that to be part of my life. That's terrible to say, but that's true.

I can't remember anything of Mum's reaction. She didn't say anything to me, but I know she had discussions with Viola. If I had said something to her, she would have responded. But I don't remember saying anything to my mother.

My father never seemed to discuss the incident much with Mum. Probably husband and wife, perhaps when they were getting ready for bed, might have discussed this.

My brother Jackie was outraged. Young men usually are, when something happens to their sisters. But his outrage wouldn't carry much weight, because he would get angry and then it would all be gone. And what could he do?

I think Mum wanted to have things cool down, considering Dad. Because he was the type that might get on the bus and go up to New Glasgow. She didn't know. He was that type. I don't think he would have, but he was always threatening to do something to somebody because of something. And my mom was his way to level things off.

Not that she didn't see the injustice. She certainly did. But she didn't want to add to Dad's fuel by sitting and discussing it in a negative way.

I don't know what Dad would say. I don't know if Mum did or didn't write a letter to the newspaper about this. And I don't know why I don't know.

Actually, I *do* know why.

I don't know because I didn't want to know. Maybe

I was going to a dance that night. I don't know what I was doing, really. I was probably going out somewhere. I sound very shallow. But I did not want to know.

I do know this: I could not have done what Viola did. I would have just gone out of the theatre. In the 1940s, I wasn't a very forceful person in getting what I wanted or in speaking out. I'm making myself out as some kind of wimp. But I didn't want it in my life. I had a good job and I did it well. And I think—I did not want to be looked upon as black. I'm black, yes, I knew I was. But I didn't want to be looked upon as black, by the people I worked with. Now that's a shameful thing to say. But I had my own world.

I didn't have any problems at work. I got along well with everybody. There were discussions at the Fisheries Lab, in the little corners of the building, about the Viola incident. I heard one say, "Who did she think she was, that she couldn't go upstairs?" I pretended that I didn't hear anything.

Instead of my going and talking to them. Well, I couldn't, because I didn't have the tools. I didn't have the complete understanding of racism. I was only nineteen years old—a young nineteen years.

It's so selfish, but I had a world like few blacks had. And I didn't want to rock the boat. I knew there were people where I worked that probably would prefer me not to be there, but they were very few. I didn't bother with them. They didn't bother with me. I had a boss who didn't see colour. And the people around me were my friends, and still are.

I certainly would never say, "Oh, that's not my

sister." But it's just that I did not want to be associated with anything racist, because it only meant trouble. And I didn't want any trouble, because I had a wonderful life.

I THINK, FOR VIOLA, the heart went out of a lot of things when this case was lost. I think she felt supported and not supported. The NSAACP was behind her one hundred percent by that time; they had a fund to help pay for the trial and lawyer, and it is said more white people than black contributed. In fact, there was money left over that supported other NSAACP initiatives, so that was certainly a good thing.

And then, her lawyer failed her, made choices that gave the judge an opportunity to quickly deny the case. The racial issues never came up. Her lawyer tried to have the original conviction quashed by using something called *writ of certiorari*. It was dismissed on a technicality.

But one of the judges, Justice William Hall, said: "Had the matter reached the court by some other method than *certiorari*, there might have been an opportunity to right the wrong done to this unfortunate woman. One wonders if the manager of the theatre who laid the complaint was so zealous because he had a bona fide belief that there had been an attempt to defraud the province of Nova Scotia of the sum of one cent, or was it a surreptitious endeavour to enforce a Jim Crow rule by the misuse of a public statute."

Also, her marriage had not been going well, and her husband Jack did not like the issue anyhow. Perhaps it didn't fit with his own business or his image as "King of Gottingen Street"—but in any case he was never happy with seeing his wife away so much, traveling for training and for business. He did not go with her to the court. Carrie Best went with her; he refused to go.

In any case, Viola started looking around for something else to do. She invested in real estate, fixing up buildings and renting them to black families. She kept her beauty business going for a few years but eventually she closed Vi's Studio of Beauty Culture and did not continue supplying her customers with her products, gave up on her franchising plans.

She left Nova Scotia, and went to Montreal. She took a course for a year, before she went to New York. A business course, not beauty culture. And in New York she tried her hand at being an agent for entertainers. That's what she was developing when she died.

I'll tell you this: I don't think Viola wanted it either—the incident in New Glasgow or the court cases that followed. She did not choose it. There are all kinds of worlds that people make for themselves, or have for themselves. She had her world that she wanted to protect, and I had mine—and when you come right down to it—Viola didn't want her world disturbed either.

I do not think that Viola was a social activist. She didn't plan to be one. Because her passion was not to right wrongs. But she was a brave and determined businesswoman—and a singular one at that.

When it was all over, she tried to get back on track.

The Nova Scotia Association for the Advancement of Coloured People wanted her to keep the issue going. They wanted to know if she would be their spokesperson. They were really moving by then. They had just gotten the first two girls into nursing school—two qualified black girls that had been refused before.

They wanted Viola to tell her story, to help promote the cause of justice for blacks. She could probably tell that story better than anyone, but she was no public speaker. She wasn't comfortable.

I remember the night of the graduation of her first class of the Desmond School of Beauty Culture. They made a big "do" of it, in the YMCA on Barrington Street. The mayor was there, and the alderman was there. There were guest speakers and musical presentations.

The girls were on the stage. Viola had given them each their rolled-up diploma. Then it was her turn to speak. She went to get a drink of water. I was there. I looked at her. "Are you all right?" I could see beads of perspiration coming out on her upper lip. "Viola, are you all right?" She whispered, "I'm not good at speaking on stage, in front of people."

I looked at her like she was somebody else. "Viola? You?" She said, "I can't—I can't do this." I said, "Yes, you can."

She went out. And she started to speak. And she used an inane expression, something like "Unaccustomed as I am to public speaking." I know she thought it was stupid when it came out of her mouth. And she halted. And then she said, "Well, I'm happy to be here because my girls worked so hard." And she got more into it. But it was a poor speech, not what you thought she could give.

Still, I don't think that fear of public speaking is what stopped Viola from going on a speaking tour about the Roseland Theatre incident and the trials. If at all, that would be only a tiny part of her thinking. It is fair to say that Viola had other goals, her eyes set on being a successful entrepreneur in black beauty culture. I think the real reason she didn't become the NSAACP spokesperson is that she hadn't finished her own dream, she wanted to achieve her goals.

She came to my father and they discussed it. He asked her, "What do *you* want to do?" And she said, "I'm halfway to where I want to be. And I've got a class of fifteen girls that have six more months of training from me before they graduate. Then I want another class."

He said, "Well, then your answer's 'No.' You've answered your own question."

AND IN 1947, she graduated her first large class of young black girls that she had taught. They went out and began working in various parts of Nova Scotia, New Brunswick and Quebec. Look at the example she set. Who is to say that by sticking to her goals, maintaining a successful beauty shop, and training other women in black beauty culture while setting very strict standards—who is to say that she was not making significant positive racial and feminist achievements—things only she could accomplish? I say she was.

If only she had not been stalled.

CHAPTER TWELVE

Finding a Home in Halifax

MY PARENTS HAD PASSED AWAY. Mum died in 1963, and Dad in 1964. And I moved. The house was put up for sale. Viola had made the down payment, and I had made the mortgage payments on the house after that. She took care of the business end of it. Eventually the city was going to expropriate our property. And I wanted to move nearer where my boys went to school, and nearer my work. I thought the South End of Halifax would be the best thing. By now the boys were attending the Halifax Grammar School, all three of them. They had been given bursaries. I wanted them to walk to school.

So I was looking for an apartment. I got one that proved good the first year—everything was working out fine—and then they upped the rent. And I was just making it then.

So, I put a notice up at Dalhousie University that

I would take a student. This is 1965. A rap on the door, and there's a girl from Jamaica. Edith. She was studying nursing administration. She was already a nurse.

I gave her my room. The boys still had their room. And I took the living room, slept on the sofa. You gotta do what you gotta do.

Edith was fine. She played the accordion, a wonderful diversion. I didn't go out that much, I didn't have the money. But I did go to Dalhousie events every now and then. They had West Indian activities going on, and she was part of that. So she would say, "Wanda, would you like to come with me? Or you go, I'll take you, and then I'll come home and take care of the boys."

She was extremely thin and extremely intelligent.

Before moving in with me, Edith had living accommodations through a brochure sent to her in Jamaica. It was on Oxford Street. When she arrived there, the woman gave Edith her own cup and saucer and plate and knife and fork and spoon. She made her put it on a tray. And she ate—and then she put the tray outside. Edith wasn't permitted in the kitchen. She told me, "I have never been treated like that in my whole life. And I didn't have any place to go."

And her a nurse.

And then somebody told Edith that this woman was looking for someone to share her apartment. So Edith knocked on my door.

She told me how she was living. "I am desperate.

I cannot live like that," she said, "I might even kill that woman!"

She was a smart lady who happened to be coloured, and she had to eat like the dog. And she came to me and she was wonderful. She lived with us for the rest of the year. I told her the apartment was hers.

And she defended us. I guess I didn't have enough backbone. One time the toilet was plugged and the boys had to go to other places for the bathroom. I told the landlord, but I guess you have to tell people with conviction when you want something done. I was paying the rent. And the kids had to go around to friends' homes to use the bathroom.

He came by for the rent. Edith let him have it. "What you think? Black people don't need to use the bathroom?"

They fixed the toilet. Edith said, "There, do you see, Wanda? You don't take no guff from those people!" And the kids liked her.

The next year, I moved again. Edith went to Toronto to take a hospital position. I was told that Dalhousie had a group of five houses all joined together on University Avenue near Henry Street. They were single family houses, all the same. Old but in reasonable repair. That was home for the next five years.

We rented the whole house. It was three bedrooms upstairs, a living room, dining room, and kitchen. But it was hard to heat. It was very drafty. And I used to buy wood—had it cut to thirteen inches, for the small fireplace in the living room. And still the boys were happy. They wanted a home.

Everything was kind of shabby inside, but it was ours. The boys could walk to school. And I walked to work in good weather.

AFTER FOUR HAPPY YEARS, I got a notice from Dalhousie in 1969, in the spring, that in six months they were tearing down the whole thing, that I had to find other accommodation. I got the notice by mail. And I thought, Well, I'm sorry to go, but in six months I can find something.

That's when the horror stories began.

The boys would come home and say, "I saw this sign on a window on South Street, 'Apartment for Rent'"—and never thought about being black. I don't think so. I mean, everybody was white. The only black people were the students. There weren't any black families in the area.

A friend from the Fisheries was driving me around. This apartment is for rent. That apartment is for rent. We'd have the newspaper in hand. I would go to the apartment listed in the paper—I circled everything—get there and they would say, "It's gone." "Rented already." Or else they'd jack up the rent. One man said to me, "You people can't pay that kind of rent." Another man said, "You married?" I said, "No, I'm divorced." "Children?" "Three children." "Oh, no. No—that's too much partying going on."

Would he assume that if I'd been white? I don't know. I mean, I have three kids, I'm alone, and I'm partying!

Meanwhile, the girl that was driving me around

was getting angrier. She's white and she's more angry than I was.

We went to a house in the South End. My friend Mabel said, "You come behind me. I'm going to knock on the door." She knocked. "You have a place to rent?"

"Oh, yes."

And then I stepped inside and said, "Well, how much is it?"

And she said, "*You* want to rent it?"

I said, "Yes, I have three children." She said that the second floor was the apartment, and there was a loft, like a large bedroom. I said, "That would be lovely for my oldest boy." The rent was fairly reasonable. Heated. And I said, "Oh, I like that."

And she said, "I'll give you the name of the lady who owns this place. You can go talk to her."

Well, this sounded promising. So we went. And within ten minutes we knocked on the door. And she opened the door—on a chain. "What do you want?"

I said, "Did the lady call to say we were coming about the apartment?"

"Oh, it's gone."

And Mabel said, "Oh, you liar!" She couldn't contain herself. "You lie!" she said.

The woman said, "I beg your pardon. My brother-in-law just decided he wants it."

"Oh," Mabel said, "give it up."

I wanted to laugh. I was angry, but I could see the effect it had on her, this white girl, when she knew this woman was blatantly lying. Firsthand, she saw the lies people tell when they see the colour of your skin. And the woman said, "Oh, it's gone! You get away from my place. How dare you? My brother-in-law is taking it." And what do you do? Maybe it was gone. Yes, and pigs fly.

Five months later, I'm still looking. I was offered a house in the North End, but—too far away. I didn't want it. And the atmosphere wasn't right for the kids. I'm away all day.

One morning I got up. It was in the summer. Kids weren't in school. I was getting ready to go to work, and one of the boys was going to baseball. I said, "Oh, look at this!"

There was a wrecking ball outside the kitchen window. There was this ball! I called work. "I think I'll be late today."

I went to the accommodations officer at Dalhousie University. Mr. Mosher. He was an older man, in his 60s maybe. He was getting ready for retirement. This is 1969. I'd never met him. We had had correspondence. I told him, "I'm at 6066."

"What?!" He said, "They're all gone! Everyone's moved."

I said, "Not me. I have no place to go."

He said, "But we've given you plenty of notice. You've had all this time."

Everybody else had gone. And all the other houses were down. They were just rubble. And I'm still in my house. And the wrecking ball is there. I was next!

I told him, "Look. I can't get a place to live because I am black, I am divorced, I have three children. Nobody will give me a place to live. I've tried. I've been trying for five months. They won't rent to me. They've told me, in not so many words, or no words, or even in the words, that it all comes down to the fact that I'm black."

He said, "That's terrible!" I'm not sure I believed him. But he said again, "That's terrible. That's not right." And I said, "No, it isn't."

"Okay," Mr. Mosher said, "I have something for you."

So he reached in the desk and took out two sets of keys.

"This is the 1248, this is the 1250 Henry Street. Each of them is vacant. Now," he said, "you go in. Take your children and look the houses over. You decide which one you want. You put your children in where you want them to go, in which rooms. Then the rest of the house is empty. I want you to rent to students. The rest of the house is for students who find it difficult to get accommodation because they are coloured or disabled. Or they look poor. Whatever reason people give—students that can't get a place, I'll send them to your place. You fill up your house. And we'll give you the place for reasonable rent."

And I said, "What is reasonable?"

He said, "$250 a month." And he said, "Charge what you like. It's up to you. That's your money. That should pay the $250 and give you some extra. You get a number of students. But take your children in first."

Before I even got set up—I didn't have any beds— they were knocking on the door. The first students they sent me were summer students. They were mostly teachers upgrading their certification, wanting more courses. Some from Truro, some from Havre Boucher, and we had some from Cape Breton. We had a girl from out west, Alberta. They just kept coming.

So I purchased two single beds. They were clean, they were nice. And I had one fold-up cot, and that was it. That was it for the house! The house was bare. We didn't have very much other than our own furniture. I managed to buy more over the next year or so.

My kids were delighted. You should have seen them running when I told them! Oh, they were happy. And they even had a basketball hoop in the yard.

It was summer. Those first students weren't going to be permanent students in the area. They could have gotten a place to rent, but they wanted my place because it was on campus. Besides, I only charged one rent. I was there from 1969 to 1975, and I charged each student the same thing for the whole time: ten dollars a week. I bought a refrigerator, a separate fridge. If they used the fridge, it was eleven dollars. An extra dollar. So I charged eleven dollars a week from each student.

The summer students really had nothing to do with what Mr. Mosher had asked me to do. And they were only going to be there for a six weeks course. But they had trouble finding a place. One student came from Frankville. Tall fellow. And very, very thin. He was a teacher. I said, "I don't have any room. I don't have a bed."

He said, "I'll sleep on the floor."

I said, "I can't have you do that. I've got a fold-up cot."

"I'll take it!"

And there he was with his feet hanging out the end of the cot! He said, "I'm fine. I'm fine. I'm fine."

IN AUGUST, I GOT A PHONE CALL from somebody in sports at Dalhousie. He came to the house. He said he knew this fellow, knew his family. And he just desperately needed something near the university. It turned out that he was disabled. And his mother was afraid of him getting refused or embarrassed. You worry about that child that's not considered okay in the world. You worry about their getting hurt and embarrassed. And he wasn't a child. This boy was twenty or twenty-one. From New Brunswick.

His name was Darren. He looked like a thalidomide child. He was white. Some people would be kind of spooky around someone like that, would feel kind of afraid—somebody with no thumbs, and somewhat shorter arms. In any case, he was visibly impaired. No thumbs, and two fingers. Just little arms coming out of his sleeve.

We had a break-in at the house. And some of his clothing was taken, his suits in particular. His father was a tailor, made all Darren's suits. He said, "I'd like to see the guy that stole my suits try and sell them downtown!"

Darren has gone on to a very successful professional life. He called us when he was promoted. There are three or four of our students that have kept in touch right to this day, what's going on in their family. Like at Christmas, or the birth of children. One of them even brought their children here for a visit.

Darren was a sweetheart. He was a nice guy. The only thing that I had to do for him that—he didn't want me to do, but I had to do it—he was the only one that went to church, every Sunday. That doesn't make him better, but I'm just pointing out that he had to get dressed up, and he had to wear a collar. So I would fasten his collar button, for his necktie. He couldn't do small buttons or anything like that. But that's the only thing.

The students took care of their own food. But then they wanted Sunday dinner. They saw how I cooked for my children. They sent Darren down to ask me, because they figured I would not say no to him! He asked me would I consider cooking dinner for the boys. They would pay me, pay for everything. I thought about it, and I said yes. I said, "I'll cook the meal, but don't pay me. Just do the dishes." I cooked and then I had nothing to do with it after. Sunday became a big day. Sunday dinner.

The house became a home for them. I wanted that atmosphere, raising my three boys. I think the atmosphere of learning affected my boys, because most of those students were serious students. They were serious in what they were doing and what they wanted to do. Their goals. And they studied. They had periods of intense study. At exam time I told them, "Study. Don't worry about the dishes, just leave them." I'd do them.

But they had breaks. They would come downstairs

and put on records or TV, talk or horse around. The house was theirs. Except my room.

For the most part, everybody got along well. We had one altercation. And I'm sorry to say, it was between two black students. West Indian students. They had a room together. They had decided, the two of them, that they would take turns cooking their own meals. They used the student refrigerator.

It turned out that they just got nasty to each other. When I got home one night, opened the door, and all I could hear was this noise on the stairs, this fighting back and forth. Everybody else had their doors closed. They didn't want any part of it.

I said, "I thought I rented this house to adults. What's going on? This is not my business, but it *is* my house."

So it was "He took my pen." "He took my shirt." And "I bought the meat, and he let it go bad in the refrigerator." "It was his turn to cook."

And I said, "Am I your mother? This is nonsense. I don't understand, but one of you will have to go."

"Well, I'm going anyway."

He left. And the other one, angry with me, started up. He reported me to the accommodations officer, for discrimination. I got a call, and I had to see the new accommodations officer. One look and he said, "*You* are discriminating?" I said, "Apparently so." He said, "Oh, for heaven's sake. I've had trouble with this fellow before. He does not need a home atmosphere. I'll find him another place."

But he blackened my name for a while. He said I

liked the white students better than the black.

On the other hand, in the second year, I got a letter from Dalhousie saying that I had done such a great job with the students—they were so happy and the rent was ideal—that they lowered my rent to $150 a month!

I didn't change anything. The students paid ten or eleven dollars a week. Just the same. It was like I got a raise!

I only had a few rules. I didn't want women staying overnight. I was trying to raise three boys. Another rule—the last one in at night, lock the door. And then when Sunday came, I said, "The kitchen is yours. I'm finished cooking. Eat what you want. I'm going in my room. Don't call me unless the house is on fire." I would catch up on my reading.

AND THEN THERE WAS WALLY. Would anybody have rented to Wally?

Because at first, even I didn't want him. I judged him. I don't like it in myself, but I didn't want him. He looked like he may have been on drugs.

When I saw Wally, I saw a little fellow who was very nervous, his hands shook, he wouldn't look at me. His clothing was clean, but it was well-worn, torn and with holes. He was older than the other students. He was just starting college. He wanted to get a degree.

Wally had been in a series of places before coming to 1250, just hanging on. Place to place. But no one would rent to him. Nobody. Nobody.

And when I saw him, I didn't want to rent to him

either. But I listened to his story. He and my brother Jackie both worked at the hospital. Jackie told him that I rented rooms to students. I said to myself, I'll give him a chance. Because, I was given chances. And also, so many times I was turned away because of my skin. Wally wasn't black.

So Wally came in. He said, "Don't worry. I'll keep my place neat." I selected his side of the room. There were two single beds. "This is your side." I gave him a little more instructions than the other boys. Keep it neat, and do this, and do that. I told him what we don't allow.

As it turned out, I didn't have to. Wally had been in the army. He had had training in how to keep a place neat. He had signed up after Grade Ten and stayed in for five years. He went back to day school after the service, and graduated from Grade Twelve. That's when he came to Dalhousie, to my place.

When he arrived he only had a few books. He had no suits, he had very few clothes. Just the bare necessities. Everything he had came in one small cardboard box. That was his luggage.

And he got up every morning, went for a run, came back, took a bath, cleaned up his room, and went off to classes.

And what became of Wally? Wally was going to be a teacher. They made fun of him. And he told me he couldn't teach. So he went into phys ed, got a degree. When he finished that, he went back in with the military as a reserve naval officer.

Wally became a chaplain—United Church ministry. He served two years in Churchill Falls, Labrador. Then he returned to the armed forces as a military chaplain. He earned his parachutist wings. He was a flying padre. He finished that and then he went into the church proper. Served different places with the church. And he went on studying. And he got his Ph.D. and served with the faculty at St. Stephen's Theological College in Edmonton. He has a lovely wife and kids.

Would you believe it? Rev. Dr. Wallace Charles Nelson Frye.

AND THEN THERE WERE THE SUNDAY DINNERS.

I had two specialties! I would buy the cheapest cut of beef, like a blade roast. The largest I could find, and the cheapest. I won't go into the recipe; it's in my head. Something I made up. With lots of vegetables: mushrooms and green pepper, celery, onions, garlic, and cooked beef. You sauté all the vegetables first, add the gravy. Then you put the cooked meat in and you simmer it for a while, then serve it on a bed of rice. That's cheap. You can feed the multitudes with that and it tastes great.

Darren always told his mother that I made veal dinner. She asked me, "I'd like to know how you made your veal dinner!" But I could never afford veal. She laughed when I told her it was beef.

My other specialty was chicken—a chicken with sauce. And rice. Or they could have baked potato. And vegetables. It was also inexpensive. You could get chicken on sale. I always cooked up enough for everybody.

I bought bread but I used to make what they call ninety-minute rolls.

And, every now and then, I would have a fried chicken dinner. Mainly for my oldest son Steve. He's a fried chicken fiend. I learned the recipe from my first husband's grandmother in the States. I could never make it like that, never tasted chicken like that, before or since. But I learned as best I could.

So everybody would eat on Sunday. I'd prepare it, and then I would be in my bedroom, after they started to eat. Have some of Sunday for myself. Because I worked all week. And they'd be laughing and talking, and sometimes you'd hear about their projects. But most of all they were carrying on, kidding each other. Then they'd tease someone about whose turn it was to do Sunday dishes.

And then the girls came. They lived next door. They could hear everything. They smelled the dinner. One of the girls was from North Sydney. She's a doctor now. They were all med students. Girls.

Anyway, one of them came over to legitimately borrow something. A can opener or bottle opener. It was Sunday.

"What are you doing?"

I said, "Well, we're having our dinner."

"You do this every week?"

"Well, just Sunday."

And of course: "Would you like a piece of pie?" I mean, she's standing looking in the doorway.

"Just a minute. I'll be back."

And she was back with a pizza pie, something like that. And tea or something. And she came back next week—would I give them Sunday dinner with the boys?

But it was "No. I can't do that. I can't stretch it any more. But you can have dessert." So after that—the girls usually came in for dessert. Dessert was pie, rice pudding, cake, or cookies. I used to make the works. It was for my kids too.

AND THE LOBSTERS! At the Fisheries Station where I worked they experimented on lobsters. I didn't work in the shellfish department, but I knew what they were doing. They had large tanks with the lobsters in them and harbour water was pumped through continually. The lobsters were separated for different experiments. Perhaps a chemical added to the water, injections for some. There was one group of lobsters left untouched—the control group. Then when the experiments were over, these control lobsters were still good to eat.

They had a list posted for fair distribution of the "leftovers" among the staff. And every time it was my turn, I'd call home: "Get the pot ready, boys, I'm coming!"

My family and the students had lobsters. They were so happy, all sitting there eating. Lots of shell-cracking and paper towels. And the phone rang. And it's Darren's mother. He had only been with us for a few weeks and his mother was concerned how he was getting along. "Tell her I can't talk now. I'll call her back. I'm eating lobsters!" So I said, "He's eating lobsters. He'll call you." And then she said, "I just called to find out how he was. Now I know. Thank you." And she hung up!

And they'd go and tell their friends, "Guess what I had last night. Lobsters! My landlady gave them to me!" Oh, we had a great feed.

AND SO THE HOUSE WORKED. Actually, it became much more than I thought it would. And it was one of the best times of my life. The hardest work—a big house and all those people. But being my mother's daughter and my sister's sister, I could take it on. Certainly my mother's daughter. She could work around the clock.

And I married Joe and he moved in, and from there on we only had four tenants. And it worked for the students who needed that house, and it worked for my boys, growing up.

CHAPTER THIRTEEN

A Walk on the Wild Side

WHEN I TELL THIS STORY, I usually ask whether anyone in the audience is a single parent—a mom or a grandmother raising a child. They'll understand what happened to me.

You get tired.

This came across to me in 1965. My children were going on a science camp from school. They were going to be away for a week. So naturally—I worked, had a full-time job—so naturally, I took that week off, because there were certain things I wanted to do. Clean up the house. Check on things. And relax. This would be my week. This would be my week to be free—"free at last, thank God Almighty, free at last."

That doesn't mean to say that I didn't love them. You know what I'm talking about, don't you? So okay: The three figures go out the door with knapsacks on their backs. "Bye, Mum." "See you, Mum." "You boys be good now." "Okay, Mum."

The bus from school pulls up. I wave, and I close the door. And I come into my bedroom. I take a deep breath. I lie down on the bed, and close my eyes.

Then I snap them open. What am I doing? Time's a-wasting. I gotta get going. I gotta get to work. Get to work! Get up! Get up! Get things done. Now, I gotta get on my working clothes. Thinking, what do I wear? There are things you can't wear when you're the mother of three boys. But today I'm not, because I'm free at last. So I rummage in my drawer, get out my shorts. And believe me, they are short. And they are holey. And I don't care, because I'm free. And I put on this blouse that has seen better days and less flesh. But I don't care. Because, I'm happy.

I'm happy I don't have to cook dinner. I don't have to look for a pair of socks. I don't have to hear: "Mum, I need a clean shirt." "Mum, would you help me with the homework?" I'm free.

So okay, I'm not quite free. I'm feeling a little— tightness. Oh, it's that bra. I reach up under and I un- snap it and I throw it up in the air, and guess where it lands. Right on the bedpost. One of the posts. It lands there, and it stays there, because I'm not picking it up. I'm not cleaning anything up.

So then, there I am: a braless wonder. Shorts that had seen better days. No bra and a loose blouse that gives me freedom to breathe. What will I do next?

So I sashay out to the boys' room, and then drag out their bureau drawers. Put them on the living room couch. As I pass Gordon's bed—he has one of those big Mexican sombreros there on the end of the bed. And it's got those little cotton balls, different colours, all hanging around the edge on little strings. I put it on my head. And I am sharp.

Oh, yeah.

So I go in the living room, and I put on a record. It's Ella singing, "Oh, the lady is a tramp." And I say to myself, "This is the life!"

So I'm sorting socks, underwear. "That one's too small. That one's too old." I wonder where those socks go when you only have one sock. Where's the other one? Is it around crying for its mate? Oh, well, it's a good sock—why is it that you get the good ones?! Now I don't know. Jeff's got to wear that. Nah, he won't like it. But he's going to have to wear it. I'm not buying any more right now.

"Okay. This pile is for Jeff. This pile is for Stephen. This pile is for Gordon." So as I'm doing this I'm thinking, "Well. I'm feeling a mite peckish." My father's expression. So I wheel my way through all the clothes and socks and bureaus. And I go to the fridge and I spy, "Aaaah! The Colonel's best"—left over from last night. So I grab the bucket, and a can of pop, and I sit down amidst all the clothes. And I start to eat with Ella singing her heart out. Aaahh. And I'm eating chicken. Chicken. Kentucky Fried.

And you know what? When you eat chicken—there's bones. What do you do with the bones? Aaah, I don't have to get up and put them anywhere. I'll just drop them on the floor. If it was good enough for Henry VIII to throw his on the floor, it is good enough for me. I toss them on the floor. And then what have I got? Greasy hands. Of course when the boys are here and they're at the table, they have napkins. You don't take your hand and wipe it across your mouth. What do I do? I'm not getting up for a napkin. I'm free. So I'm wiping all the grease on my blouse.

Oh, I feel good, and belch loudly.

Then I think, Okay, got that done. And I stand up. I look at myself in the hall mirror and I'm thinking, Mmm, I'm not bad. Need a little lipstick. I don't have much. Found it in the corner of the drawer. Get the lipstick out, put some on.

And then, do you know what I saw in the corner of the drawer? I saw a package of cigarettes. Now, I don't smoke. Never have. I don't care if you smoke or not, it's your business. I took the package out. I had them there for my brother, who visits me every week. I took one of those cigarettes out. And I said, "Well, if Bette Davis can do it, so can I."

So I put the cigarette to my mouth, and I lit it. And I'm walking around. I'm coughing but I'm walking. "Oh, good God in heaven, how do people smoke?" The tears are streaming down my eyes. I practice for a little while. I'm getting kind of good at it. And I walk out to the mirror in the hall and I look at myself.

"You hussy. You tramp. You are good." And I say, "Oh, I really feel good today."

"Now," I say to myself—greasy hands, cigarette in hand, "Okay, Wanda, you look kind of—ooo, you're hot." And I've got this sombrero on. The kids' belt slung around my waist. No shoes. I tell you, this is the life!

And, the doorbell rings.

I give one look over my shoulder like a Marilyn Monroe, and I say, "Oh, you're good." And I sashay down the hall. I say, "I am feeling great." And I open the door.

And guess who's there.

Oh, yes, it's our minister. And I say to myself, "Oh please God, take me now. Take me now." But I say to him, "Oh! Good morning, Reverend. How are you?"

He glances at me. He glances at the cigarette. I drop it on the floor, and put it out with my bare foot.

"I just came to see about Sunday."

I'm a Sunday School teacher, you know.

So he comes in the door. I start to propel him into my bedroom—forgetting that just a few days before I changed my bedroom to the living room and the living room into the bedroom.

When he goes through the bedroom door, what does he see? My bra, in all its glory. And I think he thinks, "Oh God, what have I stepped into?" And I say, "Oh, excuse me, excuse me. Here's the living room. Here's the living room, Reverend. Reverend, here's the—sit down."

And he looks around. It looks like a war zone.

"Well, don't sit there." I sort of take things off a chair. "There. Sit down."

Ella's still singing. And he says, "Would you turn that off, please?"

"Yes, yes, I will. Yes, I will."

As I go to turn it off, his eyes drop to the bones on the floor. And I take my toes and try to hide them under the clothes. It's not lost on him.

So we sit down. And we discuss this Sunday School meeting, and what's going on. And all the time we're talking, I figure there's something bothering him. The balls on my hat are shaking. As he gets up to leave, he says, "Well now—I'm so glad to see that you're still reading your Bible." Just as though to say, "Perhaps this woman can be helped. She's reading the Bible."

And I say—instead of saying, "Thank you, Reverend"—I say, "Oh, no. No, no. You see, that big big book. That's my father's dictionary. I use it for doing crossword puzzles."

And with a roll of his eyes, and an "Oh God, what is going on here. Please God, give this woman some help," he went out the door.

I come back. I'm not switching any more. I'm not sashaying down the hallway. I jump on the bunch of clothes on the sofa, and I look around and say, "Oh, God, what he must think of me. Oh Lord, what have I done? These children are going to be—what have I done? I've made a fool of myself, I look like a tramp."

Then I say, "I don't care. I don't care what he thinks. Because you know what? For one week, I'll be free. Free at last. Thank God Almighty, I'll be free."

CHAPTER FOURTEEN

I Am Not Viola

NOW I KNOW THE QUESTION people will ask me: In 1969 I was being turned down left and right when I tried to rent an apartment in the South End of Halifax. That was a long time since 1946 and the night Viola Desmond made her stand in the Roseland Theatre in New Glasgow. And I am Viola's sister. And I was being turned down because I am black. And because I was divorced and I had three kids. But mostly because I am black.

What happened to Viola, in its way, happened to me.

And even I am surprised that I was not more aggressive, that I did not even think of Viola in terms of what was happening to me.

Well, the fact is that I didn't.

And I really get annoyed with myself for not lashing out. I could give lots of examples. There was a time when Viola was home. And Dad was in bed, not well. And Mum had just passed away. Viola was there helping with Dad.

Anyway. I sent the boys to the laundromat. Our washing machine broke down on Saturday and the boys took the bags up on their wagon—the laundromat on Agricola Street. "I'll come when the laundry is done."

After a while I told Viola, "You know, those boys have been gone quite a while. I'd better go."

And just as I got to the door, the doorbell rang and a policeman came in with my boys. And the first thing Jeff said, "I didn't do anything! Mum, I didn't do it!" I said, "Well, just a minute."

Then the policeman came in, stepped in the hallway, looked up in the living room. "Do youse people live here?"

Viola was right there. "Yes, we do."

"Well, are you the mother?"

"No, here's the mother." Me.

He told me that the woman who ran the laundromat had missed her pay cheque—the money. It was stolen. And there were other people in there. But she let them leave and she told the policeman, "I know they did it. Those boys did it." She let everybody else go, and kept them there, and gave them a kind of strip search, looking for this money. She found no money.

"Well, they've probably got it in the laundry, or ditched it, or something." But they couldn't find the cash.

The kids told her, "We didn't take it." Which did not mean anything to her. Then the policeman brought them home, and warned me.

After he left Viola said to me, "Are you going to do something about that?"

What could I do? But I said, "I'm going up and speak to the woman." Viola kind of rolled her eyes.

I did go up and speak to her. I told her, "You know you let the person go that had your money. And you did not treat my children fairly, because they're coloured children."

When I got home, Viola said, "You didn't do it right."

"Well, what would you have done?"

She said, "It's done now. But I wouldn't leave it. I would have had somebody called up to pay the consequences."

But I didn't want that. It's something should have been done and I didn't do it. Viola said, "I can't do it, because you're the mother, and you should take charge." I told her I would do more. But I didn't. Call me a coward. I didn't.

I'm not a stand-up-for-my-rights person. I should be but I'm not. And I often wonder how my mother got through, with the small, almost-daily, injustices her children suffered. Not "suffered," that's not the word. Had put upon them. Little things, like the things when we'd tell her after we came home from the clinic, about the mistreatment we'd get there, and the names we were called on the school grounds.

Mum didn't retaliate like Viola. She felt at that time—and that's a long time ago, when I was small— that you have to get along in the world. Not that you have to kowtow to people. You have to remember who you are. But it's best not to do anything, if it's clearly not to your advantage.

When my brother told her, "Mum, the nurse is putting our files to the back so we have to be last. We have to wait there all day. So that's why we're not going—we're not waiting."

And Mum told us, "Yes, you are. It's not right, but you *are* going. Because you need your check-up, you need your health."

I'm sure she was as hurt, more hurt, than we were. I didn't get it then, but I get it now. I know what's going on. But as I said, I'm no Rosa Parks, or Viola Desmond. But I'd defend my children. Other than that, I didn't have their kind of gumption.

MUM ONCE LET VIOLA plead a case for her. It had nothing to do with race but it had to do with injustice. This happened while I was in the States. I found out about it because when my children and I came home, Mum had $10,000 in the bank.

Mum owned houses. She had inherited them from her father, and then she lost them one by one. Viola checked the records to find out why she lost them. And Mum said, "There's no point, I didn't seem to have the money."

Viola found out that Mum's lawyer had cheated her out of her money. Viola wanted to sue him. Mum said, "I don't think you can do anything about it after all these years."

However, Viola went to the courthouse, and she looked up records, and she did research on the houses. She discovered that the lawyer had chipped away at Mum's estate. That's why Mum wound up with nothing. Viola's contention was that Mum was a mother, and she was busy all the time. She wasn't stupid, but she just couldn't keep track of the money, where it was going. Viola said that the lawyer took advantage of Mum's situation and fixed the books.

So she brought her case to the courts against the lawyer's estate. The lawyer who was retained by the estate met Viola in the hall of the courthouse and said to her, "Where do you get your knowledge?" Because she had represented herself so well. And she said, "I got my knowledge the same place you got yours. From the legal books."

Viola won the case. It never went to court. They settled for, I think, $20,000. Viola told Mum, "I took time from my business to do this. And I'm going to take 10,000. And you put your 10,000 in the bank."

That has nothing to do with racism, but it just shows you the type of person Viola was.

CHAPTER FIFTEEN

I Fly a Kite

WHEN I WAS GROWING UP, there weren't any black girls in Guiding in Halifax. I had a daughter. She was born a few months before we moved to North Sydney in 1975. And what do you do when you have a daughter?

My son was in Scouts. And his father took care of that. My daughter had her friends in school. One day you could wear your uniform to school. "Oh, what's that?" "Well, I'm a Spark. I'm a Brownie. I'm a Guide." So Sarah came home: "I want to join the Brownies."

They met at the Anglican church, once a week. And I enrolled her. I said to myself, for an hour and a half a week, "Free at last!" I can go to the library. This is great!

I dropped Sarah off for her second meeting, just stepped in the door. I started to go, and a lady said, "Oh, Mrs. Robson, could you help me?" I said, "In what way?" "Well," she said, "there's a group down there and their leader didn't come in today. I wonder if you could help." I said, "I don't know what to do." "Oh, you'll know what to do. Don't worry about it. You just go down there. I'll be there in a minute."

And that minute turned out to be almost thirty years. I'm still there. And I'm still Guiding. I love working with the girls.

THE BROWNIES WANTED to have a kite-making project. The staff at the Alexander Graham Bell National Historic Museum offered a course in kite-making and how to fly a kite. So, we as a group—the children and the mothers—we couldn't afford to go to Baddeck. So I said I would go, and I would take the course for all of them. Then I would bring materials back and teach everyone else.

I called the museum, explained it to them. "Well," they said, "you'd have to come on a children's day, because there's no adult classes." I said, "I'm coming for the children. Could I come?" And they said, "Of course. Come."

On a bright beautiful day, I rolled up to the museum. I was wearing my Guiding uniform to identify myself, to make sure I would be admitted. And in those days I could get down on the floor. I wasn't hampered by bad knees or an aging back. I was quite excited.

A large group of children were there. Some of them had their mothers with them. Some had a teacher. But I was the only adult participating. The others stood in back, around the circle. But they were only allowed to watch; they were not allowed to assist the children.

The first thing they do, they give everybody—each child and me—a package containing the material you had to use to make your kite. We are all in a circle on our knees on the floor. I'm there. I'm on my knees. You spread out in front of you all the materials that you need. So there I was.

I noticed one thing. The children glanced at me. I didn't seem to belong, but they didn't seem to mind. But one mother did not like to see me in the circle. She didn't say anything but I felt her hostility. But I wasn't concerned. I wanted to know how to make and fly a kite. I was there to bring information back to the children. They wanted to make kites. This was one of the Guiding challenges. We were to pick a windy day. And whether it was a meeting day or not, they wanted a day that was windy. All get together if the wind was right, make our kites, and go out and fly them.

So I'm there on the floor, working away. Hey! This is not bad! I'm making a kite! It was neat! It was easy! And I'm proud. I'm not a person that's good with crafts, but when I start crafts and I do something—I'm like a kid. Did I really do that? I did! Wow!

We all stood up with our kites and went outside. We trooped out the back of the building, the little kids and me, walked out and around to the hill. I could climb a hill then! And we flew our kites. And the teacher went around to adjust our strings, make sure everybody had their kite flying right.

Now I'm standing there. Little boy beside me, his mother behind him. She kept talking to him. You could tell right away: over-protective.

Anyway. I'm there. And the wind is coming. I say, "Hey! We're gonna have a great day!" And he looks at

I Fly a Kite

me. I say, "Really!" And he's delighted. Okay. Got a partner here. He was a nice little kid.

And our kites go up!

And I said, "Look! Look!" He said, "Look at mine! Look at mine!"

Our kites are way up there now. Oh, they're up! We're all looking up. And he said, "Look at mine! Look at mine!" I said, "Boy. I think yours is higher than mine." I said, "You've done a great job." And he said, "Thank you."

And all of a sudden, our two kites are entangled. Our lines got tangled. And we tried to get them apart. The museum lady came up, and she tried. Oh, they're up there! They were flapping, and everybody was looking up, and other kids were jumping, "Look at mine! Look at mine!" And mine bumped into his. They couldn't get us undone. They dragged them in, brought our kites down.

The little boy's now telling me, "Gee, I'm sorry."

"I'm sorry too, but it's nobody's fault."

His mother comes up. And the museum lady said to the little boy, "It happens sometimes. We're very sorry. But we're going to see that you get another kite. You're not going to miss out. You come back again, and we're going to give you another one. Now you know how to make one."

The mother comes up from behind, when the museum lady went down to check on all the others. Little boy is standing there. And she said to me, "Who are you, anyway? And what are you doing here?" she said. "This is for children!"

And I said to her, "I'm a Brownie leader."

"What's that?" She shouted at me. And the museum lady down the hill heard her and looked up. "What's that?" She came up. She explained to the woman, "Well, she was given permission to come here."

"I don't care," she said. "How dare she ruin a small child's fun! Do you know how long he's been looking forward to this?"

She said, "She's here for the children."

"Did you hear me? I don't care!"

My son this and my son that.

And that little boy stood there, and he looked down. And he was getting red. He was embarrassed. I could feel his discomfort.

She told her son, "Get your things together! We're not coming back here again. This woman, who is she, anyway?"

Then she mumbled that racist word. Terrible word.

The boy looked up at his mother.

"Come along!" she said, and she's trotting off. The boy stopped for a minute. He looked up at me. I swear, I'll never forget his eyes. And he said, "She didn't really mean to be mean."

That's what he said. "She didn't mean to be mean." She called him, and he went off with her. I thought, You can learn a lesson from your little boy, kiddo.

CHAPTER SIXTEEN

Mum and Cradle World

ICAN'T SAY THIS TOO MANY TIMES: When you come from a family of fifteen children, you know that your mother's favourite word is: Share. Share. Share.

Once I saved up ten cents. Ten cents! In the 1930s! Ten whole cents. A small fortune at that time.

There was a restaurant and a bakery combined, near our home. I saw the sign on the window: Home-made Pies. And I decided, "I'll have a piece of pie all to myself!"

I crossed the street to the restaurant. And I looked around to make sure that nobody was watching me. From where my father sat reading by the window, he could see everything! You couldn't *do* anything!

So I slipped into the bakery. I looked around. My head was down, because I'm a kid and I'm doing something wrong. But I had a thirst for a piece of pie that was all mine.

"What'll you have, little girl?"

I looked up. I saw on a sign "Boston Cream Pie."

"Uh. A piece of Boston cream pie. How much is it?"

"Ten cents," he said.

"Would you put it in a bag, please, to go?"

I put the ten cents on the counter, grabbed the bag, ran down Gerrish Street and I ran along Brunswick Street. I got behind St. Patrick's School.

"Mine. All mine. A piece of pie—all mine!"

I put my hand in.

"That's not pie. This is not pie." It was strawberries or something with jam on it! But it was not pie.

I didn't know that Boston cream pie was not a pie. Boston pie is a cake! With a layer of jam in the middle! I was so disappointed. But I shoved it in my mouth anyway. It wasn't pie—didn't have flaky crust—it was cake.

But it was all mine!

So I ate it, shoved it all down my throat. I made sure there was nothing on my lips. I went home, wiping my mouth all the way. I wiped my mouth a hundred times before I got home. You never feel that you've got all the crumbs if you've been eating something you shouldn't.

I slipped into the house, sat down at the dinner table. As I had eaten the pie so fast, I could still feel it halfway down.

Mum said, "What's wrong with you?"

"Nothing. Nothing."

"Well, you're not eating your supper?"

"I'm not hungry."

My father: "Oh, Gwen, I think she's coming down with something when she doesn't want supper."

I felt so guilty. And so full. And so stupid. That I promised myself, "I will not fool them again."

OF COURSE, I COULDN'T FOOL my mother. I thought I had fooled her when I went to church each week and, week after week, I won a chocolate bar. She figured out how I did it! My mother figured it out!

At the end of the service, they would give a chocolate bar to the children who could find out from what passage of the Bible the minister's wife was reading. She'd have her book and each child would have a book, and every time she'd turn a page—she'd be talking at the same time, and she'd turn a page—every time, I'd also turn a page. And then she'd ask on what page was a certain passage—and I'd have it.

And then when I came home with a chocolate bar the third week, beaming, "Look, Mum, what I won!"—she asked, "Just what were you doing?" I said, "Nothing."

"*What* were you doing?"

And my mother had a very soft voice, she never yelled. And my sister says, "I wish she had yelled because when she gave you The Look—'Anything, Mum, but not The Look!' Not The Look!"

She gave me The Look.

I said, "Mum, but I was just following the pages."

"You mean you were cheating?"

The Look.

"You were cheating, and that's not right. Give me the chocolate bar."

She caught me every time!

OUR MOTHER WAS OUR GREAT PROTECTOR. She often wrote letters in our defense. She had written that letter to Dr. Wilder Penfield about my brother Alan.

She wrote another one about my brother Jackie after he was in the army and they were trying to deny him a pension. They had taken him in when he was seventeen, just a couple months short of his eighteenth birthday. Then they dismissed him because he got pleurisy or pneumonia or TB. And she wrote a letter telling the army, "It's your fault. He was up there in the rain putting up tents and everything. And when you took him in you passed him as A-1. And he isn't A-1 now."

So, finally, there was a bigwig from the army who came to our house. He said, "We're going to send him home from the hospital in Kentville, the sanitarium."

Mum said, "Is he well?"

They told her, "Well, he's better than what he was." And he asked her, "Where is the room that your son will have."

"I beg your pardon," she said. "He's not coming here."

They came to look at the room, and she said, "You show me where the doctors say he is all right, and I will consider it. He's not coming here. I have other family in this house. He's sick! And you did it!"

She flat out refused to take her son into the house.

And the man from the army said, "Mrs. Davis, you're right. Don't let them do that."

She said, "Of course I'm not going to do that."

And that was a woman who never went anywhere. But that was just one of the many issues she faced and resolved. She would fight. And she fought with the pen. And when Jackie came home—not only did he come home well. Mum wrote and convinced the army that Jackie was due a pension. And he got that pension! I mean, he'd only been in the army two months!

I don't know where she got that kind of strength. She was only seventeen when she got married. She never had a mother. But she was a remarkable, remarkable woman.

More than once I asked my father something—something would come up—and he said, "Why didn't you tell your mother?" This was when I was older, married. I said, "Well, what can she do?" He said, "You don't know what your mother can do." He recognized her strength.

I THINK OF MUM WHEN I REMEMBER watching Viola fight for me and my kids in Winthrop, Massachusetts. She took one look and said, "You're living like this. It's a good thing Mum doesn't know." She went about improving my situation, while I stood there saying, "I can't do anything about this."

"Yes, you can," she said. "What do you mean, you can't do anything?"

She went to the landlord, and said, "How dare you charge this much rent from this poor woman who's been taken advantage of by a man who everybody thinks is some kind of a god? And," she said, "this is not right."

And he lowered my rent! I mean, it's amazing, amazing to remember what she did. And Viola showed me how to save $200 when I was on social assistance. She told me, "You know what our mother did, on a lot less money. So, you do it." And she said, "Fortunately, your children are young."

Viola put up a list of recipes for me. And this is a woman who had no interest in cooking. We baked. Got the staples in.

"You're going to bake bread."

"I never baked bread in my life."

"Well, you're going to now."

You know what? I was proud of my bread!

But those were little things that come right back to our foundation. To our Mum.

BUT MY MOTHER WAS NOT PERFECT.

Her father was a Baptist minister. She was strictly Baptist. We were Anglican, because of Dad. When I was a baby, there was a program at the church, at the Anglican Church, called Cradle World. The Anglican minister encouraged her to go. Mum didn't want to go. She never felt comfortable in that group.

Anyway, Mum decided that she would take me

to Cradle World at the church, be with other women and their babies—perhaps in solidarity with Dad. He wanted her to go there.

So, she took me to her first meeting. And all these other mothers were there with their babies. "Oh, isn't that cute! Isn't she adorable!"

Mum immediately took offence. She grabbed up her baby—me—and went home early.

"Oh, I'm not going back."

"What happened? Did someone insult you?"

"Well, yes. Yes, they did."

Dad felt she was looking for a reason not to return!

The mothers had gathered around me at Cradle World, her baby Wanda. I had a lot of curly hair. One of the women said, "Oh! And just think!" And she ran her hand through my hair. She said, "And just think: We go to a beauty parlour to get this."

To this day, I do not find anything offensive in that.

But Mum certainly did. I think she wanted an excuse to get out of there. She wanted someone to insult her! And this was the highest insult they could come up with, to tell her that her child had this lovely curly hair—curls they had to go to a beauty parlour to get.

My father always knew when my mother meant something. "I'm not going back." And later, when I asked, "Well, Mum, what's wrong with what the woman did?" She said, "Well if you don't know, I'm not going to tell you!"

THE MINISTER CAME TO THE HOUSE and tried to convince Mum to come back to Cradle World. He sat down in the living room with her and they talked quietly. She just said, "I'll think about it." But she never went back. She never went back.

And when she did go to the Anglican church—she went back if we kids were in plays and concerts at the church. For those things she would go. But she never went to church there.

She knew that the Anglican Church was not her haven. And every now and then she would need her Baptist fix. "I'm going to church. Anybody want to come with me?" The Cornwallis Street Baptist Church. I can see her now, singing a favourite hymn or a gospel. It was as if you could feel her say: "Aaaahhhh. I'm home. Content. I'm happy. This'll keep me for another couple of weeks."

She didn't say that. But I could just feel that she was happy, to listen to a sermon, sing a hymn. Going occasionally to the Baptist church. Twice a month, maybe.

Although, something did happen to me at the Anglican Church, years later, when I was much older. I was living with my parents and children in 1960. And I came back home from church and told Mum that I had been insulted. And she said, "I knew it." She said, "I was waiting for that."

She was waiting for it! Years later! I finally got an insult!

I WAS TEACHING SUNDAY SCHOOL at the Anglican Church. My three boys were with me. When we finished Sunday School lessons we came into church, sat in a pew. A woman turned around and said to me, "I see you coming here every Sunday."

I said, "Yes."

She said, "Do you prefer coming here rather than going to your own church?"

I said, "I beg your pardon, but I've been coming here since I was five years old!"

I had been living for ten years in the States. I came back, back to the Anglican church where I had been confirmed, brought my kids to the same church—and she asked me, "Do you prefer coming here rather than going to your own church?"

That was almost it for me. But I stayed on a while, even continued to teach Sunday School—until I learned that the choir members held a special meeting to decide whether my oldest son could join the Junior Choir. They actually held a meeting.

I stopped attending after that.

CHAPTER SEVENTEEN

When Mum and Dad and Viola Died

MUM DIED IN SEPTEMBER 1963. She wasn't well in the spring of that year. She knew she wasn't well. She didn't eat very much. And she would stay in bed longer in the morning. Dad would get her up and bring her tea. She was diagnosed with cancer, was put in the hospital. She'd gotten very weak. Cancer invaded her stomach and her throat, and she couldn't speak. But her eyes were extremely expressive.

I sat with her a lot. Talked to her about the boys, how they were doing in school. And that they missed her.

They called from the hospital: Would we have a room for Mrs. Davis, who would be dismissed from the hospital? And she would have home care nurses. Dad thought that would be wonderful.

Then we got another call. She's dying. She had taken a quick turn. We all went there. They moved Mum from the ward to the room—*the* room.

Dad was there. I went in. I had never seen a person dying. She was trying to breathe. Dad was holding her hand. He had a pet name for her, he called her "Wibbsie." I don't know where it came from. "Wibbsie, I'm here. Wibbsie. You're not going anywhere."

And I could not take this any more. I ran out, got the streetcar, and went home.

An hour or so later, Dad came home. I started to apologize. He said, "It doesn't matter." He said, "She's gone." And he went in his room and shut the door.

I felt cowardly that I couldn't stay and see her suffer. I left it for him. That stays with me—not stays with me—but every now and then I think of it. Anyway, that's how she died.

BUT I SAW DAD IN HIS LAST YEAR, or maybe longer, taking his Bible to bed, where he read it every night. I think it helped him come to terms with his grief. I know he was lonely. And I wondered if he felt troubled about something. I don't know. But Mum loved him. He loved Mum. So that's all that mattered to me.

I know that Dad felt sorry. I think he was sorry that his economic life was so up and down. That was not his fault. One thing you can say, maybe they had too many children, too fast. And the pain they shared when children died, including the first child, James Reginald, and the last child, Burton Lloyd. They both lived very short lives. I'm sure that all this bothered him. I think it did.

But then again—he loved his children. All of us, really. He was very proud of the fact that I had the government job and government benefits. My mum told me that.

I never realized that he was proud of me, but Mum told me that "he doesn't find the words."

MUM DIED IN 1963. Dad was not well at the time. I worked every day, I had three kids, and my brother Jackie worked at the Victoria General Hospital. So there was nobody home to take care of Dad. And he wanted company, too. He missed Mum.

I started coming home during my lunch break to help him, but it didn't give me much time.

So Viola came home from New York and stayed for about two weeks. Then she said to Dad, "I'm going to go back and give up my apartment and clear up some business. I can take my own leave." She said, "I'll come back and give a hand here, be with you."

And the doctor was there at the time, in the house. He came to check on Dad. And Dad said to the doctor, "Would you talk to Viola. Talk to her. Tell her to go see a doctor—there's something wrong with her."

Because Viola looked pale.

The doctor talked to her in the living room. "When you come back, I suggest you get a good check-up. There may be something there."

Viola said, "Oh, I'll be fine, and I'll do that when I come back."

And she did come back. I thank the Lord for Viola. She stayed with Dad till the end. She slept in the big chair in the bedroom. There was a fireplace, and my brother Jackie made sure there was wood. He did the heavy stuff. Dad absolutely refused to have anyone from the hospital to help him.

But Viola—she never went back to the doctor.

VIOLA WOULD SAY to one of the boys, "Go in and speak to your grandfather." My son would just sit there and stare at his grandfather. My father said one day, "What is that child staring at?" He said, "Well Granddad, I just want to know if you're all right." "Well, speak," he said. "Don't just sit there, like a mummy. Just speak!"

Viola did the lunches and light meals, and a little bit of vacuuming, straightening up the house. I did the laundry on the weekend. And sometimes she would do something of Dad's that was needed—his sheets and things.

Nobody seemed to visit her. I mean, from the past. I don't even know if they knew she was there.

She had some paperwork, for her business that she had started. She had a letterhead. But she had put business on hold, since she was working for herself.

IT WAS A DIFFICULT DAY when Dad was taken to the hospital. He knew he was dying. Viola was with him, holding his hand and talking to him all the time. She would tell him how the boys were doing in school. He was very interested in the Halifax

Grammar School. He loved the idea of them being in private school.

Dad wanted to talk to me, but then he didn't seem to talk. So I said, "Dad, I'm here."

"Wanda," he said, "you've had it so hard."

"Dad, I couldn't have done it without you and Mum."

"Your Mum, what a woman. What a woman."

I said, "Dad, I'm so sorry I came home, and I brought three children with me. I'm so sorry, but I had to."

He said, "Don't cry over that. Your mother wouldn't have had it any other way."

So, I said, "I feel better."

He said, "Now, that's good." And he said, "Oh, I'd love to hear Harry sing a song." That was my brother. Dad said, "Oh"—just like that—"'My Rosary.'" It was a song.

We never did get around to talking much. All he said to me was I wasn't to be upset about being at home with three children. Because Mum, he repeated, "Your mother wouldn't have had it *any other way.*" And he emphasized that.

The last two days, Dad was in a coma. On the night that Dad was dying, the male nurse was due to go off duty. When we came, he said, "Your father is not really with us right now. But he wanted me to stay with him." And he made a joke; he said, "Your father said, 'Oh,' he said, 'you've got hands like a stevedore, so that's why I want you to stay with me! Hands like a stevedore, you can lift me up!'"

The next day I was at work, I got a call. Viola said, "Wanda, you come over right away." And Dad died two minutes after I got there. Viola was there, and my brother Jackie.

VIOLA WENT BACK TO NEW YORK. She said, "I'm going to make a go of it," she said, "this business that I've built up." She was becoming an agent for entertainers. She said she had an "in" with some people. "I've got a good hold on it now, and what I need is a small office. I'm working from home." She said, "All I need right now is one or two clients, and I'd be on the road. I'd be on my way."

After Dad's funeral, Viola said, "I'll be back again. I'd better clear up my business and—I'll leave some things here. I'll be back."

She never came back, because she died in her small apartment in New York. Dad died in 1964, September. Viola died in February of 1965.

So we really had no idea of how ill she was, or how she was feeling. We really don't know that. She died from internal bleeding.

I don't think the world knew how important a person had just been lost. I think her story was pretty much forgotten. The Roseland Theatre was not mentioned in the obituaries. Twenty years had passed.

CHAPTER EIGHTEEN

Keeping Viola's Story Alive

THERE IS REALLY NOTHING HEROIC or even exceptional in how Viola Desmond's story was rediscovered. There were always people who wanted to keep the 1946 events at the Roseland Theatre and the court cases alive—but for the most part the whole thing was forgotten.

But not completely forgotten. For instance, in 1998 American civil rights activist Rosa Parks—the woman who would not surrender her seat to a white man on an Alabama bus in 1955—came to Canada to receive an honourary degree from Mount St. Vincent University. During a question period, a young woman stood up and talked about Viola Desmond.

And then, Constance Backhouse had written a book called *Color-Coded* in 1999, with a chapter about the Viola Desmond case. She also gave a talk to law students and others at Dalhousie University. There we met writer and painter David Woods. He encouraged my storytelling and eventually we made presentations together based on black experience. David had created a play about Viola.

Meanwhile, I had gone back to college, determined at seventy-three to get my bachelor's degree. I took a course with Dr. Graham Reynolds at Cape Breton University called "The Many Faces of Jim Crow." Dr. Reynolds showed the class a National Film Board video called *Journey to Justice*. And hey, there on the screen was Viola and the story of what happened to her in 1946. It was called one of the outstanding racist acts to have happened in Nova Scotia.

My hand went up. "That's my sister up there." And Dr. Reynolds acted like he'd just dug up a treasure. He had many questions for me. He wanted me to talk to his class, to tell the story. I ended up speaking to classes in public schools.

Also, of course, there already was a scholarship in Viola's name at Ryerson University in Toronto, and they celebrate a Viola Desmond Day every year.

Certainly some people had not forgotten.

IN 2006 I WAS INTERVIEWED in North Sydney by Adrian Harewood of CBC. He stopped in New Glasgow on his way back to Toronto. He had talked there with Mayor Ann MacLean about an apology, and about putting up some kind of plaque to commemorate Viola's defiance. By now, the Roseland Theatre had become a grill and pub, so a memorial couldn't go there; but the New Glasgow Library seemed like an appropriate place for some remembrance. Adrian wrote that

Mayor MacLean listened, seemed amenable and said that she'd bring it to council. He suggested I get after her and "hold her feet to the fire."

I didn't think much would happen and I put off writing for what seemed a long time. MacLean's term was just about over anyhow. Time passed.

In 2007, Tony Colaiacovo published *The Times of African-Nova Scotians*, aspects of black history in Nova Scotia in a newspaper format. The first-page story was about the Roseland Theatre and Viola. The paper was distributed throughout Nova Scotia schools, and Tony challenged the students to make presentations of African-Nova Scotian stories in their own words.

And I wrote to the new mayor of New Glasgow, Barry MacMillan. He replied saying that it would have to go before town council—but I heard nothing more from him.

Instead, early in 2010, I heard from New Glasgow lawyer Frank DeMont. When he realized my intentions, we became friendly on the phone. He thought some recognition could be planned for Homecoming Week in August.

And then, all of a sudden, I got calls from Halifax and Cape Breton. Newspapers and radio and television. Patricia Arenburg in the *Chronicle Herald* said that Premier Darrell Dexter was considering a pardon for Viola. Minister of Justice Ross Landry contacted me and my three sisters in Montreal, about our feeling regarding a pardon. Sherri Borden Colley interviewed me for the *Chronicle Herald*. I think that really got the idea of an official apology up front.

And on April 15, 2010, Premier Darrell Dexter issued the Province of Nova Scotia's apology to the family of Viola Desmond and to all African-Nova Scotians "for the racial discrimination she was subjected to by the justice system in November of 1946." And the Lieutenant-Governor Mayann Francis proclaimed the Royal Prerogative of Mercy Free Pardon of Viola Irene Davis Desmond—something that had never before been done in all of Canada for someone who had died. The Free Pardon said unequivocally that Viola was innocent all along, that she never committed a crime, that justice was mishandled, and that she did not receive justice—that the treatment she received, as even a child can recognize, was not fair.

And children *do* recognize it. Over the years, I've had several questions from older students that showed that they were thinking, and that they understood. But I had one little boy in elementary school who asked me a question that no one had ever asked before. He was about eight or nine. And he said, "Well, the manager of the movie sort of said that Viola could sit anywhere, if she had paid the full ticket price. If you were black and paid the full price, could you go and sit anywhere you wanted after that?"

I thought, now he understood what I had been saying. I said to him, "You know, that's one of the best questions I've ever been asked."

WITH THE APOLOGY AND FREE PARDON, it was as though a little star was lit—and the story itself will never end. Because to me—because of the gravity and hopefulness of that ceremony in April—Viola Desmond's name and her achievement will last.

Some people are not happy that the word "pardon" was used at all. They insist that "A pardon is an insult when Viola did nothing wrong." But a Royal Prerogative of Mercy Free Pardon is different. It *means* that Viola was innocent. This Free Pardon process also keeps all of the court records intact, for history.

Still, I have to admit that I like the little confusion people have regarding Viola's Free Pardon, because it will always have to be explained to each generation. The story will have to be told again and again. Thinking about its meaning, peacefully talking to one another, will keep Viola Desmond alive as long as people want to share stories that can make for a better world.

IT HURTS ME, that she did not live to see that day, that she never knew what she had done for all of us. And I can't help but try to enter her mind, to ask her how she felt, living alone in New York, still trying to develop a new business, still trying to educate and better herself, likely thinking often of home and how the family was doing—the many family members she had guided and helped along the way. And I see her alone. And her dream of a successful beauty business had been stalled. No husband nearby. No children, which she wanted.

I think of Viola almost every day, perhaps more now than ever. And I see her on the apartment floor, dying alone, fifty years of age, still full of plans. A terrible and undeserved end.

No, an apology is never enough. A Free Pardon is wonderful but it speaks of an event that should not have occurred.

Now teachers and friends and families will have to tell the story of a tiny woman carried out of a movie theatre in Canada because she insisted on sitting in the whites-only section, and we will be able one day to look back at the bad old days of racism and see just how far we have come.

The Nova Scotia Apology and the Royal Prerogative of Mercy Free Pardon

PROVINCE HOUSE, NOVA SCOTIA
APRIL 15, 2010

Ross Landry, Minister of Justice:

Mrs. Desmond was an innocent woman. In 1946 the Crown made an error. And the time has come to right the wrong. This process began a number of months ago, when the town of New Glasgow contacted my office. One of Mrs. Desmond's sisters, Wanda Robson—whom I mentioned earlier, and joins us today—sent a letter to the town of New Glasgow about the injustice served to her sister. The New Glasgow mayor and legal counsel were ready to take action. This was a clear case of racism that should have never occurred, and the time had come to do something about it.

I commend the town of New Glasgow for taking on the

leadership role in working with the province on this important initiative.

From what we know, this is the first time a Royal Prerogative of Mercy Free Pardon has ever been issued in Nova Scotia. And it's the first posthumous pardon to be given in Canada. A Free Pardon is an extraordinary remedy, and is considered only in the rarest of circumstances, where the overall welfare of our society is concerned, as it was in the case of Mrs. Desmond. Such an apology and Free Pardon is appropriate.

Percy Paris, Minister of African-Nova Scotian Affairs:

Viola Desmond is often referred to as Canada's Rosa Parks. Both women have become symbols of defiance and non-compliance in their communities. Both stood their ground in the face of injustice and discrimination. And both women were arrested and charged with crimes that only those of African descent were subject to at that time.

Yet, there is a subtle difference in their stories. While Mrs. Parks was charged with violating a local ordinance when she refused to sit in the back of the bus, Mrs. Desmond was convicted of a crime similar to tax evasion. She hadn't paid the higher price required by the Roseland Theatre to sit in the white-only seats. In fact, the theatre staff refused to sell her a ticket for that section. You see, Viola Desmond violated an unwritten law. A law that, at that time, was common public policy. A law that stated without words, but with opinions and with attitudes, that she, and her brothers and her sisters of African descent, belonged to a group of "less-than's." Throughout her entire ordeal, few acknowledged that Mrs. Desmond's arrest was not a matter of refusing to pay the higher price for preferred theatre seating, but a matter of skin colour.

Viola Desmond dared to challenge the status quo. She refused to stay silent. She dared to ask questions. And, dared the greater community to accept her, and all men and all women of African descent, as equals.

And today, we are continuing to make life in this province better, by righting a wrong, by Free Pardoning Mrs. Desmond, and by making sure that all Nova Scotians know her brave story. With this pardon, we are acknowledging the wrongdoings of the past. We are also assuring Nova Scotians that all persons, regardless of race, skin colour, or creed, are equal under the law. We are reinforcing our stance that discrimination and hate will not be tolerated.

The story of Viola Desmond should not just be a symbol of hope and pride in the African-Nova Scotian community, but one that all Nova Scotians can be proud of.

Darrell Dexter, Premier of Nova Scotia:

Welcome to this historic day in Nova Scotia. I have formal remarks that I will deliver, but I want to begin by offering my apology to the family of Mrs. Viola Desmond. On behalf of the Nova Scotia Government, I sincerely apologize to Mrs. Viola Desmond's family and to all African-Nova Scotians for the racial discrimination she was subjected to by the justice system in November of 1946. The arrest, detainment, and conviction of Viola Desmond is an example in our history where the law was used to perpetrate racism and racial segregation. This is contrary to the values of Canadian society.

We recognize today that the act for which Viola Desmond was arrested was an act of courage, not an offence. The government of Nova Scotia recognizes that the treatment of Viola Desmond was an injustice. This injustice has impacted not just Mrs. Desmond during her life, and her family, but other African-Nova Scotians and all Nova Scotians who found and continue to find this event in Nova Scotia's history offensive and intolerable.

On behalf of the Province of Nova Scotia, I am sorry.

The actions of the past help future generations understand the damage done by racism. As we move forward, I want to reaffirm this province's commitment to equality for all Nova Scotians. Mrs. Desmond should be remembered as a leader for her time.

Today is righting a wrong that has left a prominent blemish on the province. Viola Irene Davis Desmond was a woman of incredible character and dignity. She was a pragmatist. But she also fought for what she believed in. Mrs. Desmond was not an activist. But she was, and remains today, an inspiration, a role model, a true Nova Scotian, and I would argue, a Canadian hero. I would have liked to have met her. Her courageous and spontaneous act of defiance on that brisk, overcast day in New Glasgow set in motion efforts to end segregation in Nova Scotia.

Viola Desmond was prosecuted, not because she committed an offence, but simply because of her race. That is wrong. And it is time to put it right.

I would like to extend a special thank you to Mrs. Desmond's family for participating in this historic event. I also want to recognize the efforts of the staff of the *Chronicle Herald* newspaper who have been instrumental in bringing awareness and attention to this important piece of Nova

Scotia's history. I also want to take the opportunity to recognize Her Honour, the Lieutenant-Governor of Nova Scotia, Mayann Francis, the Minister of Justice, Ross Landry, and the Minister of African-Nova Scotian Affairs, Percy Paris, who have all worked hard to correct this grievous wrong.

This is the first time in Canadian history that a posthumous Free Pardon has been granted. Now a Free Pardon, as was mentioned earlier, is unique. It is based on innocence. It recognizes that a conviction was made in error. There can be no doubt that a grievous error was made.

And I want to offer again on behalf of all Nova Scotians a sincere apology to Mrs. Desmond and her family for the events of November 6, 1946, and their aftermath.

Today is a time of deep reflection for all Nova Scotians. Out of that reflection comes the opportunity for action. An opportunity to ensure that history does not repeat itself. We must ensure that the name Viola Desmond and the lessons of her experience are passed on to the young people of Nova Scotia. Now I know that right across Nova Scotia today, there are students who are watching this event live on the internet. They are watching history being made. It is my hope that they, along with everyone here and those watching online, never forget the importance of this day in Nova Scotia's history. The injustice committed against Mrs. Desmond is part of Nova Scotia's history—a history that is taught in Nova Scotia's schools—a history that needs to be kept alive in our hearts.

Nova Scotians cannot and should not forget. Instead, her courage will serve as a reminder for all Nova Scotians to be vigilant and strong against racism in all its forms.

That is Viola Desmond's legacy.

Apology and Free Pardon

Mayann Francis, Lieutenant-Governor of Nova Scotia:

We gather today in Province House on what can only be described as an exceptional and historic occasion: to atone for the wrongs of the past against Viola Irene Davis Desmond.

Let us not underestimate the confluence of events about to unfold. On the eve of the visit by Her Majesty Queen Elizabeth II to Nova Scotia—who almost thirty years ago signed into law the Canadian Charter of Rights and Freedoms—we can proudly show Her Majesty how this province has worked to safeguard and protect those very rights entrusted to us. In 1999 I was appointed director and chief executive officer for the Nova Scotia Human Rights Commission. It was my responsibility to uphold the spirit of the charter, and to champion human rights and social justice in this province. It was a job I took seriously. Today, as the first African-Nova Scotian Lieutenant-Governor, representing Her Majesty in Nova Scotia, my passion for human rights continues to motivate me to promote justice and equality for all in this province.

Thus, the Royal Prerogative of Mercy Free Pardon of Viola Desmond, granted by me on the advice of the Executive Council, represents unwavering recognition of her innocence.

Viola is the most recent addition to a series of important Canadian historical figures to receive much-deserved recognition for past injustice.

Nova Scotian Jeremiah Jones was a Canadian First World War hero who fought bravely and contributed to the battle of Vimy Ridge in 1917. Just this past February, he was posthumously awarded the Canadian Forces Medallion for Distinguished Service.

Another fellow Nova Scotian, William Hall, was the first Canadian sailor and the first African-Canadian to be awarded the Victoria Cross for his gallant action with a gun crew during the Crimean War. His story lives on with the release this past February of a Canada Post commemorative stamp.

And of course, let us not forget the recent acknowledgement of Africville here in Halifax.

History is filled with tales of injustice. It is only on rare occasions, with the clarity of hindsight, and benefit of careful thought and measured reason, that a society comes together to undo the wrongs of the past. But make no mistake. It is impossible that, with the stroke of a pen and the granting of a Free Pardon, history is forgotten and the proverbial slate is wiped clean. On the contrary, this very moment in the Viola Desmond story will ensure her legacy lives on in legal journals, in newspapers, in human rights research, in political science debates, and in race relations studies.

Though much has been written about Viola, much more is yet to come. As we witness history unfold today in this very chamber, it is incumbent upon each of us to ensure its lessons are not forgotten. The undeniable link between the Lieutenant-Governor and Government House—given the historic use of the Royal Prerogative of Mercy—and Viola Desmond, is hard to ignore. This connection to the Crown, as well as the bravery of the Government and the people of Nova Scotia to atone for past wrongdoings, must be preserved for future generations. It must live on in perpetuity as confirmation of a new era of inclusiveness in Nova Scotia, and so that history is never repeated.

In the words of Nelson Mandela: "There is no easy walk

Apology and Free Pardon

to freedom anywhere. And many of us will have to pass through the valley of the shadow of death again and again before we reach the mountaintop of our desires."

NOVA SCOTIA

Province of Nova Scotia

Elizabeth the Second, by the Grace of God of the United Kingdom, Canada and Her other Realms and Territories Queen, Head of the Commonwealth, Defender of the Faith, By Her Honour The Honourable Mayann E. Francis, Lieutenant-Governor of Nova Scotia, on the advice and recommendation of the Minister of Justice and Attorney General of Nova Scotia, and by virtue of the powers in her vested and in the exercise of the Royal Prerogative of Mercy, is pleased to approve the following:

Grant of Free Pardon
VIOLA IRENE DAVIS DESMOND

WHEREAS Viola Irene Davis Desmond, born July 6, 1914, was convicted of an offence contrary to s. 8(8) of the Theatres, Cinematographs, and Amusements Act, R.S.N.S., 1923, c. 162 on November 8, 1946;

AND WHEREAS Viola Irene Davis Desmond passed away on February 7, 1965;

AND WHEREAS it is considered desirable that Viola Irene Davis Desmond be posthumously granted a Free Pardon from that offence;

NOW THEREFORE it is hereby ordered by virtue of the powers in me vested in the exercise of the Royal Prerogative of Mercy we do hereby grant a FREE PARDON to VIOLA IRENE DAVIS DESMOND from conviction entered on November 8, 1946 for an offence contrary to s. 8(8) of the Theatres, Cinematographs, and Amusements Act, R.S.N.S., 1923, c. 162.

IN TESTIMONY WHEREOF we have caused these Our Letters to be made Patent and the Great Seal of Nova Scotia to be hereunto affixed.

Her Honour, The Honourable Mayann E. Francis
Lieutenant Governor of Nova Scotia

At Our Province House, in the Halifax Regional Municipality, this 15th day of April in the year of Our Lord, Two Thousand and Ten and in the 59th year of Our Reign.

By Command.

Provincial Secretary
Minister of Justice and Attorney General

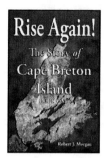

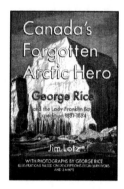
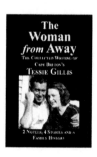